Quilting
with Donna Dewberry

©2005 Donna Dewberry

Published by

kp books
An Imprint of F+W Publications

700 East State Street • Iola, WI 54990-0001
715-445-2214 • 888-457-2873

Our toll-free number to place an order or obtain
a free catalog is (800) 258-0929.

Library of Congress Catalog Number: 2004098424

ISBN: 0-87349-897-6

Designed by Sharon Laufenberg
Edited by Nicole Gould and Susan Sliwicki

Printed in the United States of America

Acknowledgments

Many people made this book possible.

Julie Stephani, acquisitions; Niki Gould, editor; Kris Kandler, photographer; Sharon Laufenberg, designer; and Susan Sliwicki, editor; were instrumental in orchestrating the production of this book at KP Books.

Joyce Robertson, Springs Industries, was invaluable for recruiting the designers and quilters, as well as providing the fabrics and always having a vision. Maribel Delgado, my assistant from One Stroke, provided the instructions for the painting projects.

We are especially indebted to the quilt and project designers: Marsha Evans Moore, Julie A. Olson, Michele Crawford, Amy Tallent, Cheryl Adam and Ann Greer.

Special thanks go to Collins for quilting notions and Prym-Dritz Corp. for the cutting tools.

Dedication

I dedicate this book to Mom and Nanny, my grandmother, both of whom have passed away.

I am so thankful for the wonderful memories I have of both of these beautiful, amazing women. I know that they each played a part in the person I am today. They helped to inspire me at a young age and to instill in me the love for creating beautiful things.

I also must include a message and dedication to all those ladies at church who gave me the drive to not give up while teaching them to quilt. I truly can say that I learned something from each of them, as I hope they did from me. Many of them are very dear and longtime friends. I want them to know that sharing that time with them has blessed my life. Ladies, we did it; we learned to quilt!

Table of Contents

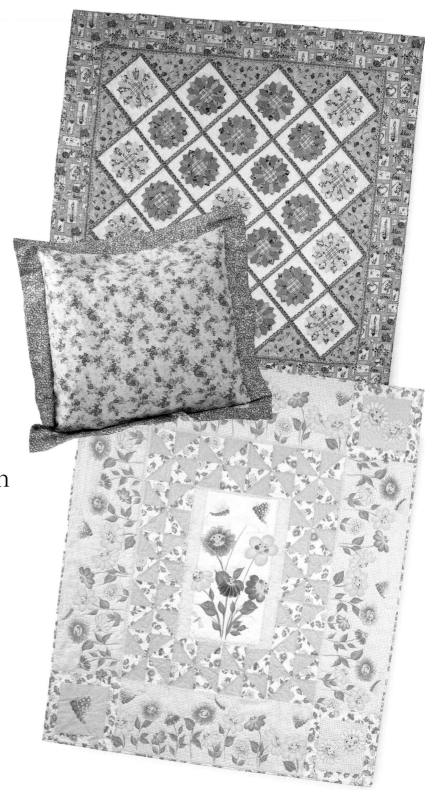

Introduction

My mother and my grandmother, Nanny, always loved fabric. They were what you would call die-hard "Fabric-holics." They spent a lot of money and time — lots of time — shopping for fabrics to sew into dream projects someday.

They taught me to love sewing and collecting. I continued that love as I made almost all of the clothes I wore in junior high and high school.

I sometimes miss the weekends going to the fabric stores. We would go into town from our home in the Florida Outback to go fabric shopping.

After I got married, I started sewing décor pieces for my home, and I created many beautiful accents. I even made matching mother/daughter outfits for my first daughter and me. What a joy that was! Soon after, I started making baby quilts, and then I advanced to teaching quilting classes at our monthly church events for women for 13 years. I helped each lady find her inner talent — and even quilt something.

While reminiscing about the days that have passed, I am pleasantly reminded of the amazing bonds of mothers and daughters. I have four daughters of my own, and now I have five granddaughters. I am amazed at how this captivating legacy will carry on.

To all of you who have that special bond with a mother, daughter or sister, you must embrace it. Enjoy every second, whether it is shopping, sewing or painting late nights at your kitchen table. These are the times you will hold within your hearts forever. The love and time I had with my mother and Nanny I now can carry on with my daughters and granddaughters. I hope to share and teach each of them something they will carry on. I know that I, too, can learn something from each of them.

My dream to share my love for creating with others has come true, and I am so very thankful. I am reminded each time I have the privilege to meet a new creative person that I have the ability to share these talents and ideas. I am so thankful for the opportunities I have to meet so many wonderful people.

"Quilting With Donna Dewberry" has brought back so many wonderful memories, and I hope my experiences and memories inspire each and every person who picks up this book.

I've had a wonderful experience working on this book. I am amazed at all of the creative and talented hands that contributed to and shared in this project. With this in mind, I would love to give special thanks to several people:

• Thanks to Julie Stephani and David Lewis for "Quilting With Donna Dewberry." I am so blessed by their friendship! Thank you!

• Thank you to Laura Farson and Niki Gould for their time, dedication and organization. They made this book far more than I ever thought it could be! Also, I appreciate the special week they spent working day and night on the finishing touches. I never will forget your efforts!

• Thank you, Joyce Robertson, for your vision and your willingness to always make it happen. I am looking forward to a wonderful future.

• I want to give a huge thank-you to all of the wonderful ladies who have shared their quilting ability and worked with my fabric. Thank you for sharing your talents on my behalf.

With all of this in mind, please know that as you flip through the pages in this book, it was created with love and hard work. Use this book to create your own masterpieces, and share that time with someone special.

In closing, I hope this book will become a welcome addition to your library of creative ideas, that you will use it for many years to come, and most importantly, that you will share it with others!

Love
Donna

Chapter

Getting Started

Tools and Supplies

Here are some of the tools and supplies you will need when creating the projects in this book.

- Iron
- Ironing board
- Pins
- 45 mm rotary cutter
- 6" x 24" ruler for use with rotary cutter
- 18" x 24" cutting mat
- Scissors
- Paper-backed fusible web
- Appliqué pressing sheet (optional)
- Batting
- Template plastic
- Sewing machine and machine needles
- Bobbins
- Sewing machine walking foot or dual-feed feature for quilting
- Hand sewing needle
- Fabric-safe marker

Basic Techniques

Several techniques and guidelines are used repeatedly for projects in this book. Refer to this section for pointers during projects.

Binding

Make the Binding

1. Cut binding strips to the size directed in the project.
2. Place two binding strips' ends, right sides together, at a 90-degree angle.
3. Use a ruler and fabric-safe marker to draw a diagonal line from the upper left corner to the lower right corner.
4. Sew diagonally on the line.
5. Trim the fabric ¼" from the stitching.
6. Repeat Steps 2 through 5 until all of the binding strips are joined.
7. Press the seams open.

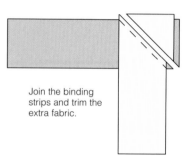

Join the binding strips and trim the extra fabric.

Bind the Quilt

1. Position the binding on an outer edge of the front of the quilt. Make sure the binding and quilt are positioned with right sides together. Start the binding away from a corner.
2. Begin stitching 2" from the end. Sew just to ¼" from the corner.

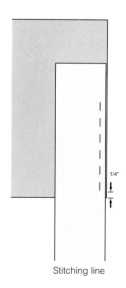

1/4"

Stitching line

Miter the Corner

1. At the corner, fold the binding strip at a 45-degree angle. The right side of the binding strip will be facing up.

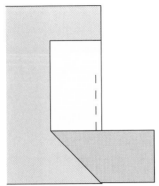

Fold the corner.

2. Refold the strip onto itself so that it turns the corner. The binding strip will be face down on the corner folds.

3. Sew the binding strip to the next side of the project.

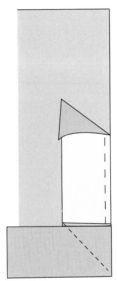

Sew the second fold.

4. Repeat Steps 1 through 3 for the remaining corners.

5. Fold the beginning loose end over at a 45-degree angle. Finger press.

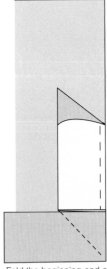

Fold the beginning end at a 45-degree angle.

6. Overlap the end of the binding on top of this angled piece.

7. Lift the end, and trim the extra binding from the lower binding piece at an angle, leaving ¼".

8. Sew through all of the binding layers.

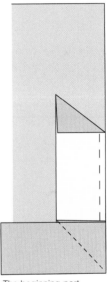

The beginning part meets the end.

Finish the Binding

1. Fold the binding around the edge to the back.

2. Turn the raw edge of the binding over upon itself.

3. Fold the binding again. Pin it in place.

4. Sew along the fold.

Raw-Edge Appliqué

Use this fusible web technique for flower, vine and birdhouse appliqués.

1. Cut out the motif. Be sure to leave extra fabric margins.

2. Apply paper-backed fusible web to the wrong side of the fabric.

3. Cut out the motif on the outline of the design. If the design does not connect the entire motif, leave a "bridge" of fabric to keep the motif whole. This is especially important for the vines that twist around birdhouse in the Shower Curtain project in Chapter 6.

4. Arrange the motifs in the desired pattern on the section of the project where they will be placed.

5. Once you are satisfied with the arrangement, peel off the backing paper. Stick the pieces to the background.

6. Use an iron to fuse the pieces; follow the manufacturer's instructions. Avoid reheating areas. Instead, make a section of the arrangement, then fuse all of the pieces at once.

Alternate method

1. Arrange the pieces on a nonstick appliqué pressing sheet.

2. Transfer the group of pieces to the project all at once, then fuse.

Seam Allowance

The seam allowance for all projects in this book is ¼", unless otherwise noted.

Templates

Template designs are given in exact sizes. Trace the template onto opaque template plastic. Add a ¼" seam allowance when instructed. Cut the template plastic carefully to maintain its exact size. If necessary, recreate the template if it gets distorted.

Chapter

The Bedroom

Dresden Plate Quilt with pillows and shams.
Quilt size: 93½" square, which fits a queen-size bed.
Designed by Cheryl Adam.

Dresden Plate Quilt

I love this quilt for a guest room. But it fits great into a master bedroom, too. I loved using a garden-themed fabric for a drop on the sides before the bed skirt. Find a fabric with several coordinates; it will add to your fun as you quilt and add accessories to the room.

Materials

- 3½ yd. Picket Fence Large Patches print
- 2¾ yd. 108" wide cream solid
- 3¼ yd. white on white print
- 2½ yd. small floral stripe
- 1⅝ yd. green daisy floral
- 1 yd. Large Butterflies print
- ⅔ yd. yellow solid
- ⅝ yd. blue solid
- ⅝ yd. rose solid
- ⅓ yd. blue plaid
- Queen-size batting, 90" x 108"
- Thread

Tip: Cut sashing and borders lengthwise to avoid joining seams.

From	Cut
Small floral stripe	8 strips, 1½" x 90", cut to yield: • 32 strips, 1½" x 12½" 2 strips, 1½" x 90" 2 strips, 1½" x 73" 2 strips, 1½" x 76"
Large Patches print	2 strips, 9¼" x 93½" (cut parallel to selvage) 2 strips, 9¼" x 43" (cut along width of fabric) 10 selvage-to-selvage strips, 2" wide

Large Butterflies print	128 blades (use Dresden Plate Blade Template)
	6 squares, 18¼" x 18¼", cut in half diagonally to yield:
	    • 12 triangles
	2 squares, 9⅜" x 9⅜", cut in half diagonally to yield:
	    • 4 triangles

White-on-white print	25 squares, 12½" x 12½"
Green daisy floral	72 blades (use blade template)
Yellow solid	72 blades (use blade template)
Rose solid	64 blades (use blade template)
Blue solid	64 blades (use blade template)
Blue plaid	25 circles, 4" in diameter

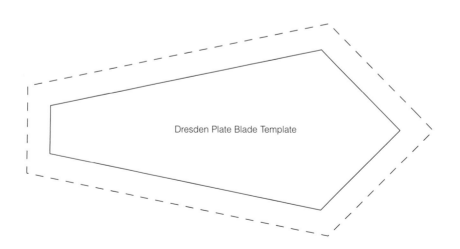

Dresden Plate Blade Template

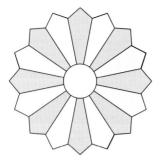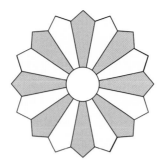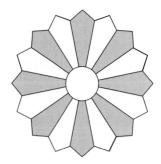

Dresden Plate diagrams

Sew

Dresden Plate blocks

1. Select eight yellow blades and eight green daisy floral print blades.

2. Sew the blades into a plate, alternating the solid and print blades.

3. Match one blue plaid center circle to the plate.

4. Place the assembled plate onto a 12½" white square. Pin in place.

5. Turn under the outer raw edges of the plate. Press.

6. Topstitch the plate along the outer folded edges.

7. Turn under ¼" along the raw edges of a blue plaid circle.

8. Place the circle over the center of the plate. Pin.

9. Topstitch along the folded edge of the circle.

10. Repeat Steps 1 through 9 to complete nine yellow plates.

11. Select eight blue solid and eight blue butterfly blades.

12. Repeat Steps 2 through 9 to complete eight blue plates.

13. Select eight rose solid and eight blue butterfly blades.

14. Repeat Steps 2 through 9 to complete eight rose plates.

Alternate Triangles

1. Arrange the Dresden Plate blocks in diagonal rows, as shown in the photo.

2. Place the large triangles cut from the butterfly print squares at the end of the rows. Place the small triangles at the corners, as shown in the photo.

3. Sew the 1½" x 12½" sashing strips between the blocks.

4. Sew the blocks into rows.

5. Sew the long sashing strips between the rows.

6. Sew the rows together.

Inner Border

1. Sew one 1½" x 73" floral stripe strip to each of the opposite sides of the pieced center panel.

2. Repeat Step 1 for the two remaining sides, but use the 1½" x 76" strips.

3. Press.

Outer Border

1. Orient one 9¼" x 42" strip and one 9¼" x 29" strip in the same direction. Sew them together to create a 9¼" x 76" border panel.

2. Repeat Step 1.

3. Position both 9¼" x 76" pieced border panels so the print is oriented vertically. Sew one border panel to the top of the pieced center panel, and sew the other to the bottom of the pieced center panel.

4. Repeat Step 3 for the remaining sides, but use the 9¼" x 93½" border panels.

Finish

1. Layer the back, batting and top pieces.

2. Quilt as desired.

Bind

1. Join the 2" wide patch print strips.

2. Bind the quilt. Refer to binding directions in Chapter 1.

Valance

It's easy to sew a custom-fit valance. Simply measure the window, double its width and cut fabric to that length.

Materials (For a 36" window)
- 2 yd. Picket Fence Large Double Border print
- Thread

See Chapter 10 for instructions.

Decorator Table Cover

A coordinating fabric table cover helps pull a room's look together without a lot of effort.

Materials
- 2 yd. Small Packed Hydrangeas print
- Thread

See Chapter 10 for instructions.

Basic/ Flange Pillows

Make your bed an inviting retreat with piles of these quick-to-sew pillows.

Materials for Basic Pillow

- 1 yd. gold solid
- Pillow form or fiberfill
- Thread

See Chapter 10 for instructions.

Panel Pillows

Set the tone for your room with panel prints and your favorite coordinating fabrics.

Materials for Panel Pillow

- 17" printed square
- ½ yd. coordinating fabric
- Pillow form
- Thread

See Chapter 10 for instructions.

Pillow Sham

Add flair to a standard-size pillow with a
coordinating pillow sham.

Materials
- 2 yd. Large Butterflies print
- Thread

See Chapter 10 for instructions.

Chapter

The Porch

Purple Porch Throw, shown with a coordinating pillow.
Throw size: 48" x 60".
Designed by Cheryl Adam.

Purple Porch Throw

This Trip Around the World quilt features appliqué accents on its borders.

Materials

- 2 yd. purple solid
- 2 yd. muslin
- ½ yd. lavender plaid
- ½ yd. dark purple floral
- ½ yd. light lavender floral
- ½ yd. Large Packed Roses print
- Thread
- 3 yd. olive green single-fold bias tape, ½" wide
- 2 yd. batting, 45" wide
- ½ yd. paper-backed fusible web

From	Cut
Lavender plaid	4 selvage-to-selvage strips, 4½" wide
Light lavender floral	4 selvage-to-selvage strips, 4½" wide
Dark purple floral	4 selvage-to-selvage strips, 4½" wide 6 selvage-to-selvage strips, 1½" wide 6 selvage-to-selvage strips, 2" wide
Large Packed Roses print	Apply paper-backed fusible web to the back of fabric before cutting out shapes. Leave extra fabric around each shape. 2 large flower clusters 4 large red roses 2 white roses 15 leaves
Purple solid	2 strips, 8½" x 50" 2 strips, 8½" x 62"

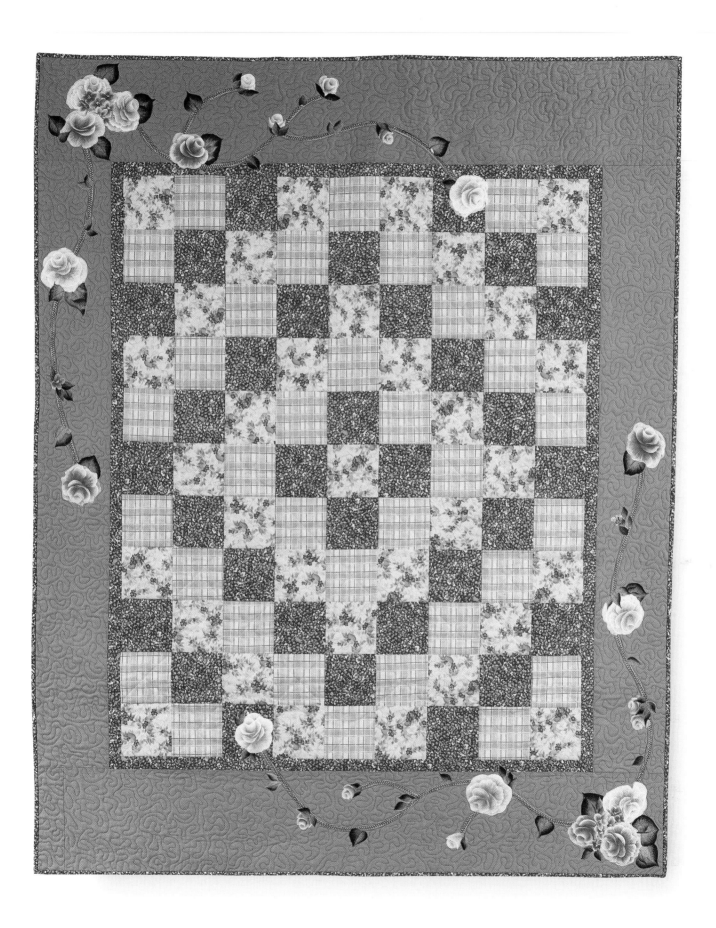

Assemble

Center Panel

1. Group the 4½" wide strips into four groups of three strips each.

Strip-pieced group.

2. Lay the strips out lengthwise using the following sequence: light floral, plaid, dark floral.

3. Sew one group of three strips together lengthwise.

4. Repeat Steps 2 and 3 for the remaining strip sets.

5. Cross cut the strips sets into nine sections that each are 4½" wide.

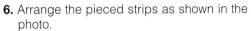

Cross cut strip.

6. Arrange the pieced strips as shown in the photo.

7. Stitch the groups together in rows.

8. Stitch the rows together.

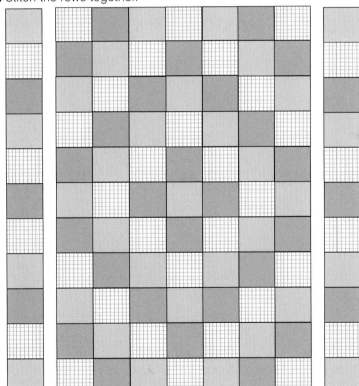

Assembly diagram for checked rows.

Borders

1. With right sides of the fabric together, sew one 1½" wide border strip to each of two opposite sides of the assembled top.

2. Press the border to the right side.

3. Repeat Steps 1 and 2 for the remaining two sides of the quilt.

4. With right sides together, stitch one 8½" x 50" border strip on each of two opposite sides of the assembled top.

5. Press the border to the right side.

6. Trim the excess border fabric so it is even with the center panel.

7. Sew one 8½" x 62" border strip to each of the remaining two sides.

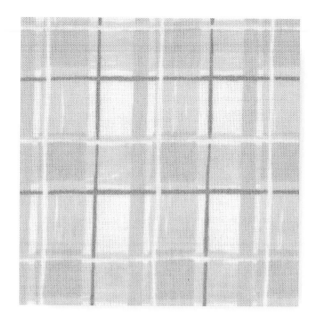

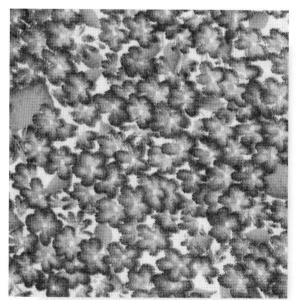

Appliqué

Flowers and Leaves

1. Remove the backing paper from the fusible web already attached to the flower and leaf cutouts.

2. Position the flowers and leaves on the larger outer border, as shown in the photo.

3. Place the olive green bias tape between the leaves and flowers to form the stems.

4. Tuck the raw edges of the bias tape under the flowers and/or leaves. Pin in place.

5. Fuse the flowers and leaves to the quilt. Follow the manufacturer's instructions.

6. Topstitch ⅟₁₆" from both edges of each of the bias tape stems.

7. Stitch ⅟₁₆" in from the raw edges of the flowers and through the centerline of all of the leaves.

Bind

1. Join the six 2" wide dark purple strips.

2. Bind the quilt. Refer to Chapter 1 for more information on binding.

Finish

1. Layer the back, batting and top pieces.

2. Stipple the wide outer border, using a meandering stitch as desired.

3. Stitch the squares in the ditch.

4. Quilt diagonally through the center of the squares.

Panel/ Flange Pillows

Mix and match pillows for a welcoming look.

Materials for one pillow

- One 19½" square panel print
- Pillow form or fiberfill
- Thread

See Chapter 10 for instructions.

Decorator Table Covers

A floor-length 70" tablecloth and a 36" square topper add drama to an ordinary side table.

Materials

- 4 yd. lavender floral fabric
- 1 yd. purple hydrangea print
- Thread

See Chapter 10 for instructions.

Chapter

Daybed Diversion

Stars and Fences quilt.
Quilt size: 76" x 94", slightly larger than a standard twin-size quilt.
Designed by Julie Olson.

Stars and Fences Quilt

This unusual block setting makes the stars float in the sky over the pretty picket fences.

Materials

- 4⅔ yd. Picket Fence Large Double Border print
- 2½ yd. muslin, 108" wide
- 2 yd. pink floral
- 2 yd. blue sky print
- 1¼ yd. green floral
- 1 yd. blue plaid
- ⅓ yd. green daisy print
- 1 Picket Fence Pillow Panel
- 90" x 108" batting
- Thread

From	Cut
Pillow Panel	To measure 16½" square.
Pink floral	3 selvage-to-selvage strips, 2½" wide, cut to yield: • 34 squares, 2½" x 2½" • 4 rectangles, 2½" x 4½" 20 squares, 2½" x 2½" 5 selvage-to-selvage strips, 1½" wide, cut to yield: • 112 squares, 1½" x 1½" 9 selvage-to-selvage strips, 1½" wide 9 selvage-to-selvage strips, 2" wide
Green floral	2 selvage-to-selvage strips, 2½" wide, cut to yield: • 4 rectangles, 2½" x 4½" • 24 squares, 2½" x 2½" 9 selvage-to-selvage strips, 1½" wide 2 selvage-to-selvage strips, 8½" wide, cut to yield: • 8 squares, 8½" x 8½"

From	Cut
Blue sky fabric	3 selvage-to-selvage strips, 1½" wide, cut to yield: • 56 squares, 1½" x 1½" 7 selvage-to-selvage strips, 2½" wide, cut to yield: • 56 rectangles, 1½" x 2½" • 8 rectangles, 2½" x 6½" • 4 rectangles, 2½" x 4½" • 4 rectangles, 2½" x 8½" • 28 squares, 2½" x 2½" 7 selvage-to-selvage strips, 4½" wide, cut to yield: • 24 rectangles, 2½" x 4½" • 10 rectangles, 4½" x 8½" • 4 rectangles, 4½" x 6½" • 2 rectangles, 4½" x 16½" 1 selvage-to-selvage strip, 12½" wide, cut to yield: • 4 strips, 2½" x 12½" • 2 rectangles, 6½" x 8½"
Green daisy print	2 selvage-to-selvage strips, 2½" wide, cut to yield: • 4 rectangles, 2½" x 4½" • 24 squares, 2½" x 2½"
Blue plaid	1 selvage-to-selvage strip, 2½" wide, cut to yield: • 8 squares, 2½" x 2½" • 9 strips, 2½" x 40"
Double Border print	2 equal-width lengthwise strips, 4⅔ yd. long, cut to yield: • 2 rectangles, 14" x 74" • 2 rectangles, 14" x 93"

Assemble

Flying Geese Sections For Outer Points: Small Pink Stars

1. Draw a diagonal line on the wrong side of the 1½" pink squares.

Draw a diagonal line on the pink square.

2. With right sides together, match a 1½" pink square to the right half of a 1½" x 2½" rectangle of blue fabric.

Sew on the diagonal line.

3. Sew on the diagonal line.

Open the triangle and press flat.

4. Open the triangle and press.

5. On the wrong side, trim the extra fabric ¼" from the stitching.

6. Repeat Steps 1 through 5 for the left half of the rectangle.

Sew the second square to the left side.

7. Repeat Steps 1 through 6 for the remaining blue rectangles.

Open the second triangle flying geese unit.

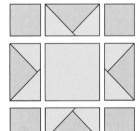

Sew the small stars.

8. Sew the stars together as shown, using a 2½" pink square for the center, four Flying Geese units, and four 1½" blue squares for the outer corners.

9. Repeat Step 8 for the remaining small stars.

10. Set 10 small stars aside.

11. For the remaining four small pink stars, sew one 2½" x 4½" blue sky border rectangle, two 2½" x 6½" blue sky border rectangles and one 2½" x 8½" blue sky border rectangle to the four sides of the stars in the order as shown.

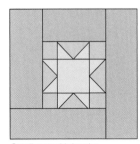

Small star with border.

Flying Geese Sections For Outer Points: Large Pink Stars

1. Draw a diagonal line on the wrong side of each 2½" pink square.

Draw a diagonal line on the pink square.

2. With right sides together, place one pink 2½" square on the right side of one 2½" x 4½" blue rectangle.

3. Sew on the diagonal line, as shown in the illustration.

Sew on the diagonal line.

4. Press the triangle open.

Press the right-side triangle open.

5. Trim the extra fabric from the wrong side, ¼" from the seam allowance.

Sew the second square on the diagonal line.

Press the left triangle open.

6. Repeat Steps 1 through 5 for the left side of the blue rectangle.

7. Repeat Steps 1 through 6 for the remaining Flying Geese sections.

Center Squares

The center squares of the large stars are made of two Flying Geese units, but this time, the colors are reversed — blue squares and pink rectangles — from those in the star point sections. For more information, refer to the illustrations included in the Flying Geese sections.

Flying Geese block with the color reversed.

1. Draw a diagonal line on the wrong side of each 2½" blue square.

2. With right sides together, place one blue sky 2½" square on the right side of one 2½" x 4½" pink rectangle.

3. Sew on the diagonal line, as shown in the illustration for Step 3 of the directions for Flying Geese sections.

4. Press the triangle open.

5. Trim the extra fabric from the wrong side, ¼" from the seam allowance.

6. Repeat Steps 1 through 5 for the left side of the pink rectangle.

7. Repeat Steps 1 through 6 for the remaining sections.

Large Star Assembly

1. Arrange two center Flying Geese sections and four outer star point sections with four 2½" blue sky squares as shown in the diagram.

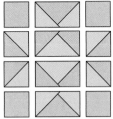

2. Sew the large pink star pieces into rows.

3. Set the pink star rows aside.

Star assembly arrangement.

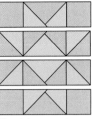

Sew into separate rows.

Four Large Green Stars

1. To create the four large green stars, repeat Steps 1 through 7 for the Large Pink Stars. Note the differences in color arrangement for the outer points.

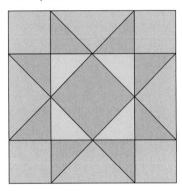
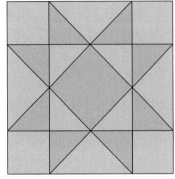

Completed large stars.

2. Sew the pieces into stars.

Section A

1. Sew one 4½" x 8½" blue rectangle to the outside of each of the large green stars.

2. Sew one 6½" x 8½" blue rectangle to the bottom quarter of a pink star,

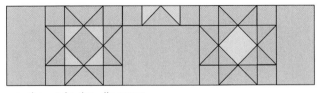

as shown in the diagram.

3. Sew the large star sections to each side of the center quarter star section.

Section B

1. Sew one 6½" x 12½" blue rectangle to the short end of a center section of a large pink star, as shown in the diagram for Section B.

Section C

1. Sew the top two quarter sections to make half of a large pink star.

2. Sew one blue 4½" x 8½" rectangle to the top of the half large star.

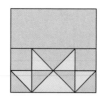

Detail of the center of Section C.

3. Sew one 4½" x 8½" blue rectangle to both sides of the center section created in Step 2.

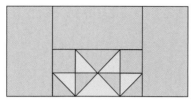

Center with added rectangles.

4. Fold one 8½" square in half diagonally. Finger press. Unfold the square.

5. With right sides together, place the 8½" square on one of the rectangles as shown.

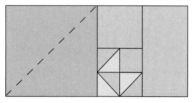

Green square on center of Section C.

6. Sew diagonally on the fold line.

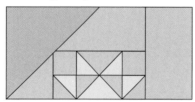

Green triangle.

7. Press the triangle open to the right side.

8. On the wrong side, trim the excess fabric ¼" from the seam.

9. Repeat Steps 5 through 7 for the second, opposite triangle.

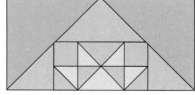

Two green triangles.

10. Sew a small pink star (with border) to the triangle ends of this unit.

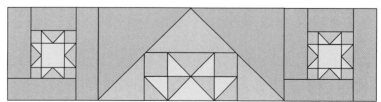

Completed Section C.

Join the Sections

1. Match the points at the bottom of the large square of Sections A and B. Pin.

2. Sew Section B to Section A.

3. Match the center square to the bottom section of the large pink star.

4. Sew Section C to the joined Sections A and B.

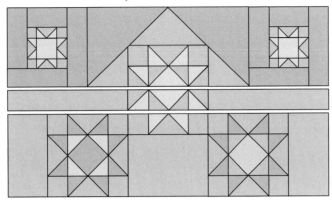

Join Sections
A, B and C.

Prepare Duplicate Sections A, B and C

1. Repeat the steps in Sections A, B and C to complete the upper section of the quilt top.

2. Set these two large joined sections aside.

Section D

1. Sew one 4½" x 6½" blue sky rectangle to both sides of a small pink star.

2. Sew one 4½" x 16½" rectangle to the star assembly.

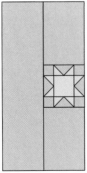

Section D star and rectangles.

3. Fold an 8½" green square diagonally. Finger press. Unfold.

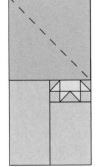

Green square on the star assembly.

4. With the right side down, place the green square on the star assembly as shown.

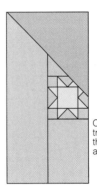

One green triangle on the star assembly.

5. Sew on the diagonal fold line.

6. Open the triangle and press.

7. Trim the extra fabric from the back, ¼" from the seam line.

8. Repeat Steps 3 through 7 for the second green square.

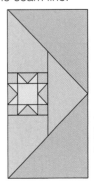

Two green triangles on the star assembly.

Section D (continued)

9. Repeat Steps 1 through 8 for the second Section D.

10. Sew the two D Sections to the center panel.

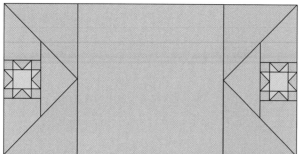

Mirror two D Sections.

Completed Section D.

11. Join one completed ABC unit to the top and bottom of Section D.

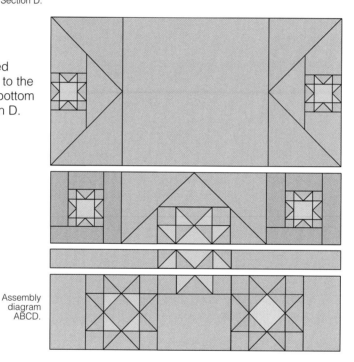

Assembly diagram ABCD.

Inner Borders

1. Sew one 1½" pink selvage-to-selvage strip lengthwise to one 2½" plaid selvage to selvage strip.

2. Sew one 1½" green selvage-to-selvage strip to the open side of the plaid strip.

3. Repeat Steps 1 and 2 for the remaining pink, plaid and green strips.

4. Cut the strip sets created in Steps 1 through 3 as follows: two 32" lengths; two 50" lengths; two 40" lengths; and two 57" lengths.

5. With right sides together and the pink edge to the inside, stitch one 50" length of the strip-pieced border to each of the two long sides of the assembled top. Press open.

6. Attach small pink star corner blocks to the 32" long strip-pieced inner border strips. Measure the short-side length before sewing the corner blocks.

7. With the pink edge to the inside, sew the corner block strips to the two short sides of the assembled top.

8. With the right sides of the green strips together, sew the two 57" lengths to each of the two long sides of the inner border. Trim sewn strips even with the corner blocks. Measure the short-side length before sewing the corner blocks.

9. Sew two small star corner blocks to each end of the two 40" strip-pieced borders. Before sewing the corner blocks, measure the short-side length.

10. With the green fabrics right sides together, sew the corner block strips to the two short sides of the inner border.

Outer Border

1. With right sides together, center one long outer border strip along one long side of the pieced top. The border will extend evenly beyond both ends of the top for the mitered corner. Pin.

2. Sew along the pinned edge, ending ¼" from the corner.

3. Repeat Steps 1 and 2 for the remaining long side.

4. Center a short border fabric strip along one of the short sides of the pieced top. Pin.

5. Sew along the pinned edge, ending ¼" from the corner.

6. Repeat for the other side.

7. Miter the corners by folding the extra border fabric at a 45-degree angle.

8. Sew along the 45-degree fold.

9. Trim the extra fabric ¼" from the stitching.

Quilt

1. Place batting between the assembled top and the muslin.

2. Stitch "in the ditch" of the seam lines to secure the layers.

3. Outline the motifs with quilting stitches.

4. Fill the open areas with leaves and flowers.

Bind

1. Join the 2" wide pink strips end to end.

2. Bind the quilt. Refer to Chapter 1 for detailed directions.

Basic Pillow

Plump up your bed with some of these easy 14" x 14" pillows.

Materials
- ½ yd. Small Packed Hydrangeas print
- Pillow form
- Thread

See Chapter 10 for instructions.

Pillow Shams

Try these shams to add tailored flair to a bedding ensemble.

Materials
- 2 yd. print
- Thread

Refer to Chapter 10 for instructions.

Panel Print Sham

Ruffled edges and a panel print fabric set this sham apart.

Materials
- 27" x 32" Picket Fence Large Double Border print
- ½ yd. print
- Thread

See Chapter 10 for instructions.

Valance

Extend a decorating theme with a matching valance at the window.

Materials

- Fabric cut to a length equal to two times the width of the desired window, and cut to a height of 12" to 18"
- Thread

See Chapter 10 for instructions.

Decorator Table Cover

Create a softer look — and instant storage — with this flowing fabric cover for a round side table.

Materials

- 2 yd. Small Packed Hydrangeas print
- Thread

See Chapter 10 for instructions.

Chapter

The Nursery

Donna's Wall Hanging/Quilt.
Quilt size: 30" x 38".
Designed by Donna Dewberry.

Donna's Wall Hanging/Quilt

Yarn ties give this baby quilt an old-fashioned touch.

Materials

- 1¾ yd. solid white fabric
- 1 Flower Party Quilt Panel
- 1 yd. batting, 45" wide
- 1 skein fine-weight lime-green yarn
- Thread
- Large-eye sewing needle
- Chick Stencil: Happy Faces 19588
- Folk Art® Paints in Light Yellow 918, White 901, School Bus Yellow 736, Burnt Umber 462 and Sunflower Paint 432
- One Folk Art® Scruffy™ Brush No. 1172

From	Cut
Solid white fabric	3 selvage-to-selvage strips, 6½" wide, cut to yield: • 2 strips, 18" long • 2 strips, 38" long • 1 rectangle, 30½" x 37½"
Quilt Panel	1 panel, 18" x 26"

Assemble

Paint

1. Stencil the chick motif onto the four 6½" wide solid white border strips. Follow the manufacturer's recommendations.

Sew

1. Sew one 6½" x 18" chick border strip to the top edge of the center panel.

2. Press.

3. Sew one 6½" x 18" chick border strip to the bottom edge of the center panel.

4. Press.

5. Sew one 6½" x 38" chick border strip to each side of the center panel.

Quilt

1. With the right sides of the fabric together, match the back and top fabrics.

2. Place the batting on top of the top layer of fabric.

3. Use a ½" seam allowance to stitch around the outer edge. Leave a 4" opening.

4. Turn the fabric right sides out.

5. Stitch the opening closed, either by hand or machine.

6. Use 6" lengths of yarn to tie the quilt every 10".

Flower Patch Baby Quilt.
Quilt size: 48" x 55".
Designed by Michele Crawford.

Flower Patch Baby Quilt

Pinwheels dance around the center bouquet of this baby quilt.

Materials

- 2⅛ yd. backing
- 1¼ yd. Flower Party Small Tossed Flowers print
- 1¼ yd. Flower Party Decorator Double Border
- 1 yd. Flower Party Quilt Panel
- ⅝ yd. green solid
- 52" x 60" batting
- Thread

From	Cut
Quilt panel	1 inside motif panel, 14½" x 21½" (fussy cut) Remaining panel border to yield: • 2 daisy motif squares, 7¼" x 7¼" • 2 butterfly motifs 7¼" x 7¼"
Green solid	4 selvage-to-selvage strips, 4½" wide, cut to yield: • 28 squares, 4½" x 4½"
Tossed Flowers print	6 selvage-to-selvage strips, 2¼" wide 4 selvage-to-selvage strips, 2" wide 4 selvage-to-selvage strips, 4½" wide, cut to yield: • 28 squares, 4½" x 4½
Double border	4 strips, 10¼" x 45", cut to yield: • 2 strips, 28½" long • 2 strips, 35½" long

Assemble

Pinwheel Blocks

1. Draw a diagonal line on the wrong side of each green square.

2. With right sides together, match a green 4½" square to a 4½" Tossed Flowers square.

3. Sew a ¼" seam on each side of the drawn line.

4. Cut on the line to yield two pieces.

5. Open both pieces. Press the half-square triangles flat.

6. Trim the "ears" at each corner.

7. Repeat Steps 1 through 6 for the remaining squares.

8. Sew four of the triangle squares into a pinwheel block as shown.

9. Trim the block to measure 7½" square.

10. Repeat Steps 8 and 9 for remaining blocks.

Draw diagonal line on wrong side.

Stitch ¼" on both sides of the drawn line.

Assemble the Pinwheel Block.

Center

1. Sew two sets of four pinwheel blocks each into two separate long rows.

2. Sew two sets of three pinwheel blocks each into two separate short rows.

3. Sew the two short pinwheel block rows to the long sides of the center panel.

4. Sew the two long pinwheel block rows to the top and bottom of the center panel.

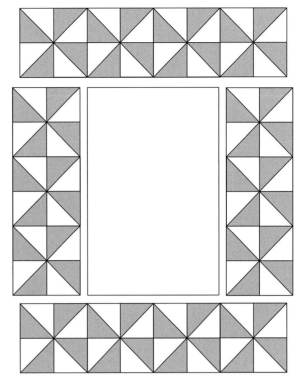

Pinwheel block arrangement.

Pinwheel row assembly.

Corner Blocks

1. Sew one 2" wide Tossed Flowers strip to each of the four sides of the 7¼" corner blocks.

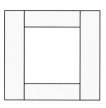

Corner block diagram.

2. Sew one corner block to each end of both 28½" outer border strips. Note the direction of the print so the flowers face upward along the border.

3. Sew one 35½" border strip to each of the long sides of the center panel strip.

4. Sew the border strips that contain the corner blocks to the top and bottom of the center assembly.

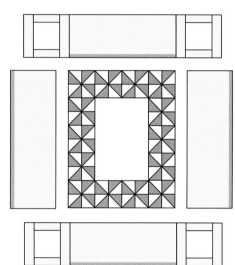

Assembly diagram.

Quilt

1. Layer the back, batting and pieced top.

2. Quilt in the ditch of the seam lines.

3. Quilt the center area by outlining the flowers and pinwheels.

4. Quilt the border by outlining the flowers, daisies and butterflies.

Bind

1. Join the 2" wide Tossed Flowers strips end to end.

2. Bind the quilt. Refer to Chapter 1 for instructions.

Crib Dust Ruffle.
Size: 24" x 48", plus 18" drop.

Crib Dust Ruffle

This dust ruffle fits over the springs and drapes under the mattress. The corners are left open to fit around the crib rail mechanism.

Materials

- 1⅓ yd. muslin, 45" wide
- 4 yd. Flower Party Decorator Double Border
- Thread

From	Cut
Muslin	1 rectangle, 24" x 48"
Border print	2 rectangles, 18" x 48" 2 rectangles, 18" x 96"

Assemble

Base Layer

1. Hem the bottom and two sides of each of the four border-print rectangles.

2. Make two parallel lines of loose basting stitches along the raw edges of the four rectangles.

3. Pull the basting stitches to gather the fabric. The gathers should reduce the fabric to approximately half of its original length.

4. Match the 96" gathered rectangle along the 48" side of the base piece, matching right sides together. Pin the pieces in place.

5. Stitch the pieces together. Use a ½" seam allowance.

6. Repeat Steps 4 and 5, matching the other 96" strip to the 48" side.

7. Match one of the 48" strips to one of the 24" sides of the base.

8. Stitch the pieces together. Use a ½" seam allowance.

9. Repeat Steps 7 and 8 for the other 24" side.

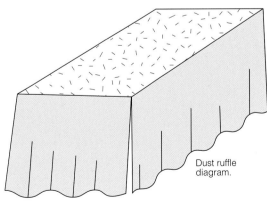

Dust ruffle diagram.

Crib Sheet.
Size: 23" x 46", which fits a standard crib.

Crib Sheet

Materials

- 1⅔ yd. Flower Party Small Tossed Flowers print
- 1 yd. elastic
- Thread

From

Tossed Flowers Print

Cut

1 rectangle, 36" x 56"

Assemble

1. Form the corners. Cut a 6½" square from each corner, as shown.

Diagram of sheet.

2. With right sides together, match the edges of the "V" formed in one corner. Pin. Repeat for the other three corners.

3. Sew the four corner seams.

4. Divide the elastic into four 8" long strips.

5. Center the elastic at each corner. Pin.

6. While gently stretching the elastic, wrap the raw edge of the fabric around the elastic. Pin.

7. Turn the hem between the elastic. Pin.

8. Sew the hem around the bottom, stitching through the elastic at each corner.

Posie Pot.
Size: 5½" x 6" x 21".

Posie Pot

Materials

- ¼ yd. Flower Party Small Tossed Flowers print
- ⅛ yd. pink gingham
- ¼ yd. Flower Party Decorator Double Border
- ¼ yd. fusible fleece, 45" wide
- 7 green chenille stems
- One silk daisy or sunflower with large leaf
- Thread

From	Cut
Pink gingham check	1 selvage-to-selvage strip, 2½" wide
Tossed Flowers print	1 rectangle, 7" x 20" 2 rectangles, 7" x 8"
Double Border	1 yellow large flower face* 2 yellow medium flower faces* 2 pink medium flower faces* 1 white small flower face* 1 lavender small flower face* 7 leaves* (*Leave extra fabric margins.)

Assemble

Posie Pot

1. Fold the 2½" wide pink gingham strip in half lengthwise.

2. Fold ¼" the strip's raw edges to the inside. Press.

3. Topstitch along the folds of the handle.

4. With the fabric right side out, fold the 7" x 20" rectangle in half crosswise.

5. Fold one top raw edge of the tossed flower rectangle over 4" to the outside.

6. Fold this 4" flap back onto itself to form a cuff. Pin.

7. Repeat Steps 2 through 6 for the other raw edge.

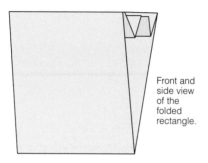

Front and side view of the folded rectangle.

8. Refold the tossed flower rectangle so that the right sides are together and the folds that form the cuff are inside.

9. Sew the two side seams.

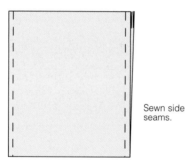

Sewn side seams.

10. Turn the piece right side out.

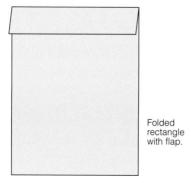

Folded rectangle with flap.

11. At the bottom folds, push the side seam in by 1" to form a pleat on each side. Pin.

12. Sew across both pleats.

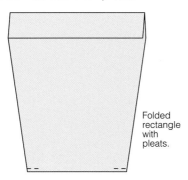

Folded rectangle with pleats.

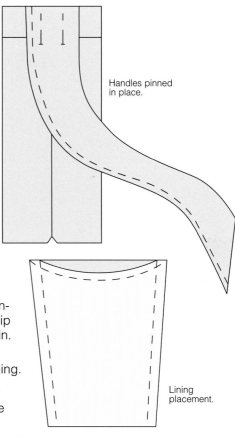

Handles pinned in place.

13. On the right side of the outside piece, center the handles over the side seams. Pin.

14. Match the two lining pieces, right sides together. Pin.

15. Sew along the long sides of the lining.

16. Match the side seams (under the handles), placing right sides together. Slip the outside piece inside the lining. Pin.

17. Sew along the top edge, stitching through the outside piece and the lining.

18. Turn the lining right side out.

19. Press the seam allowance toward the lining.

Lining placement.

20. Stitch through the lining and the seam allowance.

21. Fold the bottom seam allowance of the lining to the inside.

22. Topstitch on the fold.

23. Push the lining to the inside.

Posies

1. Place fusible fleece on the wrong side of the fabric flowers and leaves.

2. Fuse the flowers and leaves to the fleece, following the manufacturer's directions.

3. Cut the flowers along the outside lines.

4. Glue one flower and one leaf to one chenille stem.

5. Repeat Step 4 for each flower and leaf pair.

6. Arrange the flowers in a group.

7. Twist the chenille stems as a group around the silk flower stem.

8. Insert the flower arrangement into the Posie Pot.

Button Pillow

A flower button adds a playful touch to a Basic Pillow.

Materials

- ½ yd. solid fabric
- 1 Flower Party Quilt Panel border square
- Thread
- Fusible fleece
- Button
- Pillow form

See Chapter 10 for instructions.

Valance

Get a coordinated look without a lot of effort with this easy-to-sew valance.

Materials

- Length of Flower Party Decorator Double Border 12" to 18" tall and twice as long as the window width
- Thread

See Chapter 10 for instructions.

Chapter

The Bath

Shower Curtain size: 73" x 75",
which fits a standard shower curtain rod.
Designed by Amy Tallent.

Shower Curtain

Light and airy birdhouses lend an outdoor feel to your bath.

Materials

- 2⅛ yd. Picket Fence Large Double Border
- 2⅛ yd. blue plaid
- 2⅛ yards green daisy print
- 2 Picket Fence Pillow Panels
- ¼ yd. dark brown solid
- 1 fat quarter of purple batik
- 1 fat quarter of brown batik
- 1 fat quarter of white solid fabric
- 1 fat quarter of medium brown fabric
- 2 yd. paper-backed fusible web
- Clear and coordinating thread

From	Cut
Large Double Border	6 strips, 15½" x 77", with the selvages left intact
Blue plaid	1 length of fabric, 45" x 75"
Green daisy print	1 strip, 27" x 75"
Pillow Panels	8 border sections; leave extra fabric around each section
Paper-backed fusible web	1 strip, 6" x 40"
Brown solid	1 strip, 6" x 40"

Assemble

Shower Curtain

1. Hem the border strip along the bottom edge. Turn the selvage up 1"; topstitch in place.

2. Match one edge of the blue plaid fabric with the top edge of the border fabric, placing right sides together. Pin. Stitch a ½" seam.

3. Fold 2½" of the green daisy print over lengthwise along the selvage.

4. Topstitch along the edge of the fold and 2" from the fold along the top edge. Press.

Buttonholes

1. Place ½" long vertical buttonholes along the top fold in the green daisy print, starting 1" in from both sides and adding a buttonhole every 6".

2. Repeat Step 1 until you have a total of 12 buttonholes.

Upper Section

1. With right sides together, match the raw edges of the blue plaid piece and the green daisy piece.

2. Pin. Stitch the seam. Press.

3. Hem the vertical raw edges of the sides by turning the raw edges under 1". Fold the raw edge under by ½". Topstitch along the second fold.

Birdhouses

Note: Do not add a seam allowance to any of the birdhouse templates.

1. Transfer the birdhouse designs from the patterns on pages 72 through 75 to the paper side of fusible web.

2. Cut the designs apart, leaving ¼" margins.

3. Apply the fusible web pieces to the backsides of the corresponding colors of the four fat quarter birdhouse fabrics.

4. Cut along the solid outside lines.

5. Use a nonstick appliqué sheet to assemble each birdhouse with its roof pieces.

Posts

1. Apply the 6" x 40" strip of fusible web to the wrong side of the solid brown fabric strip.

2. Cut four 1½" wide selvage-to-selvage strips. Cut the strips to yield:

- Two lengths of 24"
- One length of 25"
- One length of 27"

Vines

1. Apply fusible web to the wrong sides of the vine and flower cutouts.

2. Cut along the fused vine and flower motifs, keeping the length intact by creating fabric "bridges" between the leaves and flowers.

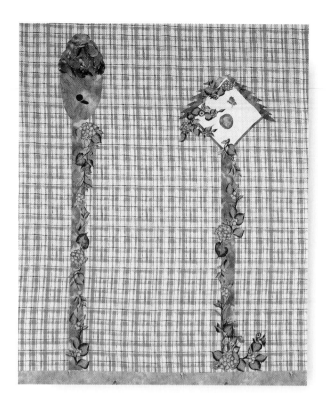

Birdhouse placement

1. Divide the shower curtain into fourths by folding it in half lengthwise and in half lengthwise again.

2. Lightly finger press the folds.

3. Position the posts, birdhouses and vines on the blue plaid fabric. Vary the heights of the posts, and evenly space the elements by using the folds as guidelines.

4. Remove the backing paper from one design at a time. Fuse the design to the shower curtain, following the manufacturer's instructions.

5. Repeat Step 4 for the remaining birdhouses.

6. Use clear polyester thread to topstitch along the fabric edges.

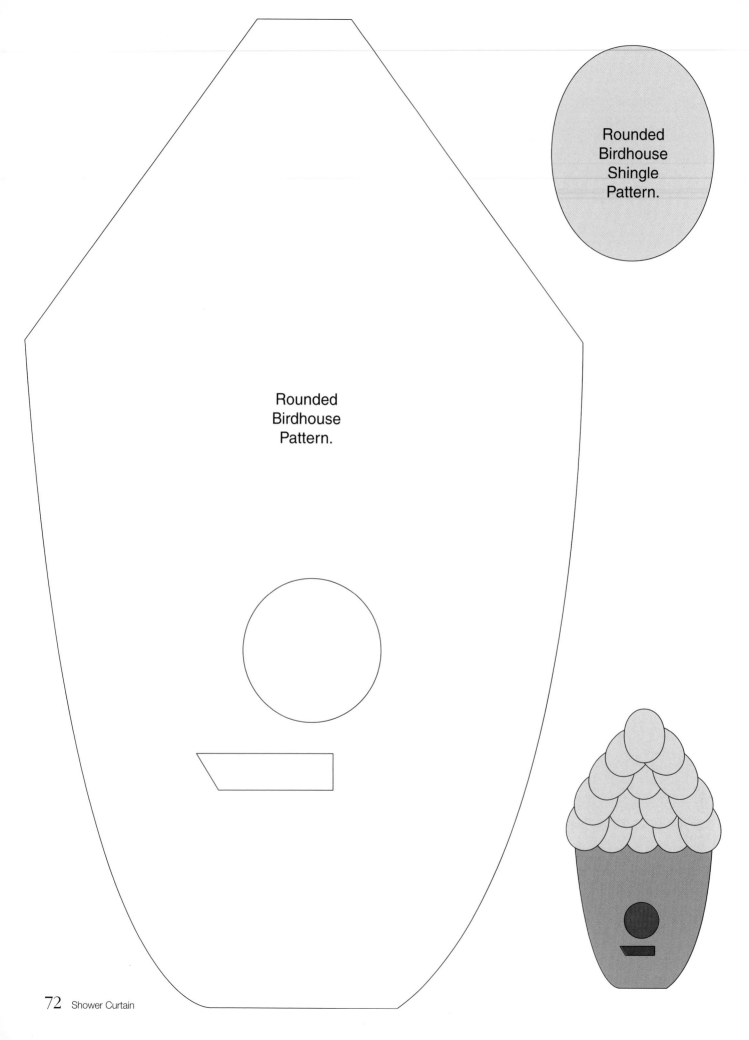

Rounded
Birdhouse
Shingle
Pattern.

Rounded
Birdhouse
Pattern.

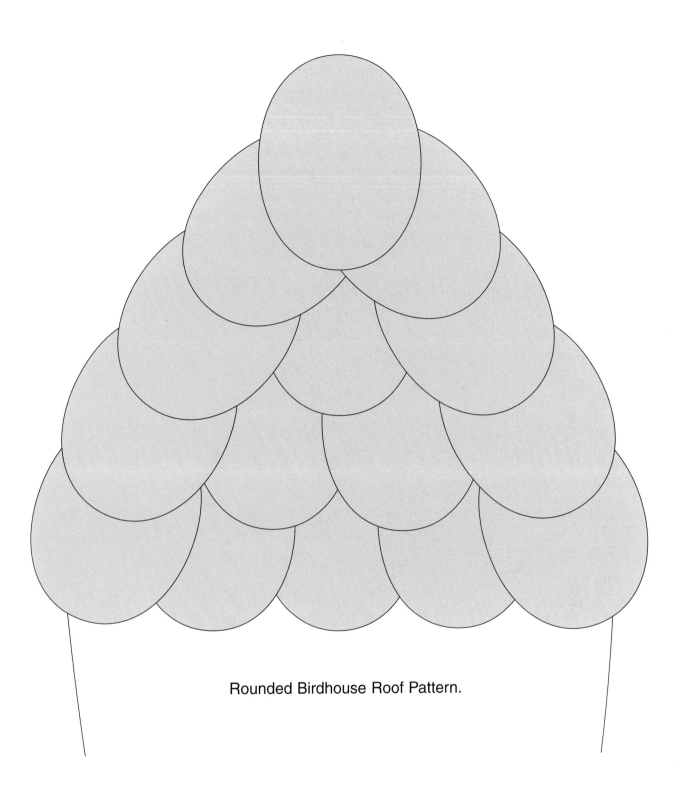

Rounded Birdhouse Roof Pattern.

Roof.

Roof.

Diamond-Shaped Birdhouse Pattern.

Bottom.

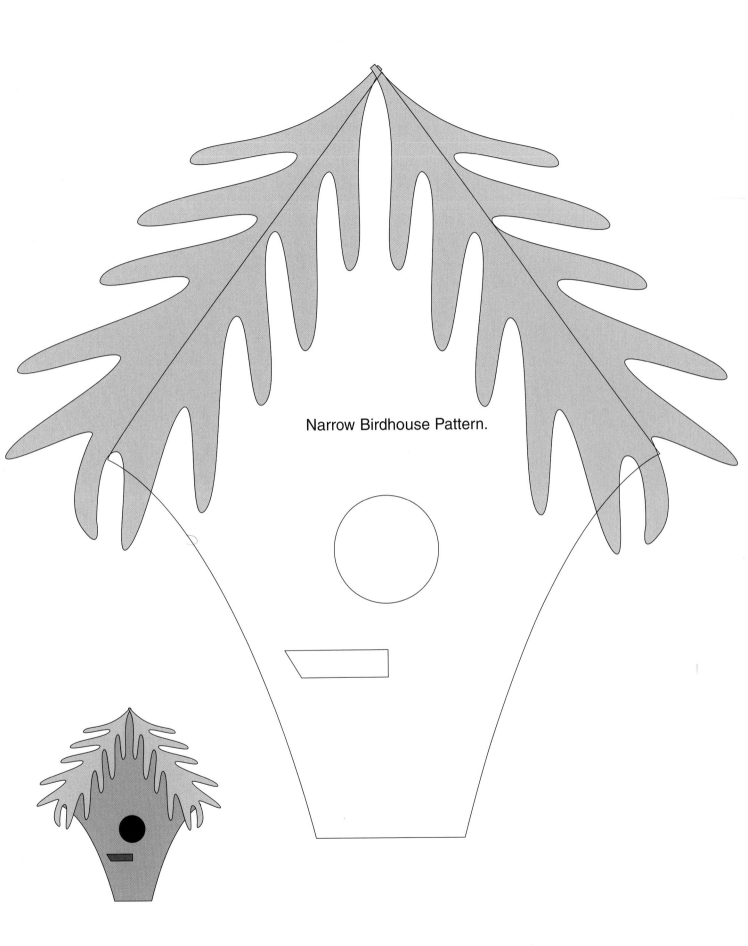

Narrow Birdhouse Pattern.

Towel Accents

Dress up your bath towels to match the birdhouse-themed shower curtain. Flat-woven hand towels are suited to this fusible web appliqué technique.

Materials

- 2 large terry cloth bath towels
- 2 flat-woven hand towels
- 1 yd. light blue plaid
- ½ yd. Picket Fence Large Double Border
- ½ yd. paper-backed fusible web
- 2 yd. light blue satin ribbon, 1" wide
- Thread

From	Cut
Light blue plaid	6 selvage-to-selvage strips, 3¼" wide
Picket fence print	2 vine and flower and birdhouse motifs (cut generously around each motif)

Assemble

Bath Towel

1. Join three 3½" wide blue plaid strips end to end.

2. Hem the short ends and one long side. Use a serger or rolled hem.

3. Place the light blue plaid right side up on the right side of the towel. Position it at the bottom edge of the towel.

4. Pleat the light blue plaid; use the vertical plaid lines as guides. Pin in place.

5. Place the light blue ribbon on top of the raw edge of the pleats. Pin.

6. Stitch along both edges of the ribbon, sewing through all layers of the pleats and the towel.

7. Repeat Steps 1 through 6 for the second bath towel.

Hand Towel

1. Apply fusible web to the wrong side of the flower and vine birdhouse cutouts.

2. Cut along the edges of the motifs.

3. Remove the backing paper from the motif.

4. Center the motif on the hand towel.

5. Press the motif to fuse it to the towel. Follow the manufacturer's directions.

6. Use clear polyester thread to topstitch along the margins of the motif.

7. Repeat Steps 1 through 6 for the other hand towel.

Chair Pillow

Create an inviting seat with this lofty cushion.

Materials
- ¾ yd. green flower print fabric
- Thread
- 20-ounce package of fiberfill
- Long upholstery needle
- Two shank buttons
- Pencil and string

See Chapter 10 for instructions.

Fabric-Covered Tissue Box

Add a finishing touch to the bathroom with a coordinating tissue box.

Materials
- ⅜ yd. fabric
- 1 box of tissues
- Craft glue

Assemble
1. With right side up, wrap the fabric around the tissue box.
2. Cut a slash along the top opening.
3. Fold the fabric inside the top opening. Glue along the raw fabric edges.
4. Fold the fabric around the sides, like you would to wrap a package.
5. Trim the excess fabric. Glue fabric in place.
6. Trim the bottom edge, leaving ½" to wrap to the bottom. Glue in place.

Chapter

The Kitchen

Garden Maze Wall Hanging.
Size: 48" square.
Designed by Cheryl Adam.

Garden Maze Wall Hanging

The lattice effects created in this clever design
are reminiscent of a garden trellis.

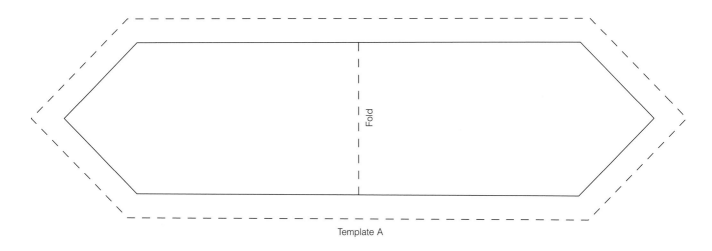

Fold

Template A

Materials

- 3 yd. muslin
- ⅔ yd. purple solid
- ⅝ yd. all-over fruit print
- ½ yd. leafy print
- ½ yd. beige solid
- ¼ yd. green and purple plaid
- 4 fruit panels, 11" square
- 52" square piece of batting
- Thread

From	Cut
Fruit panels	4 squares, 10¾" x 10¾", center panel
All-over fruit print	8 selvage-to-selvage strips, 1⅝" wide 9 Template A pieces 18 Template B pieces
Beige solid	4 selvage-to-selvage strips, 2¾" wide 36 Template C pieces
Green and purple plaid	2 strips, 2" x 37" 2 strips, 2" x 40½"
Purple solid	6 selvage-to-selvage strips, 2" wide 5 selvage-to-selvage strips, 1" wide, cut to yield: • 2 strips, 36½" long • 2 strips, 37½" long • 8 strips, 10¾" long • 8 strips, 12¾" long
Leafy print	2 strips, 4½" x 40½" 2 strips, 4½" x 48"

Assemble

Center Blocks

1. Sew one 1" x 10¾" purple strip to each of two opposite sides of a 10¾" fruit panel square.

2. Sew one 1" x 12¾" purple border strip to each of the remaining two opposite sides of the fruit panel square.

Corner Blocks

1. Sew two beige Template C triangles to one Template B floral piece.

2. Repeat Step 1 for all of the Template B floral pieces.

3. Sew these completed triangles to center Template A piece to complete a corner block.

Sashing Strips

1. Sew one 1⅝" wide all-over fruit strip to each of the long sides of one beige strip.

2. Repeat Step 1 for all of the beige strips.

3. Cross cut the strips sewn in Steps 1 and 2 into 12 sets of 11¾" long sashing strips.

4. Assemble the wall hanging in vertical rows, as shown in the diagram.

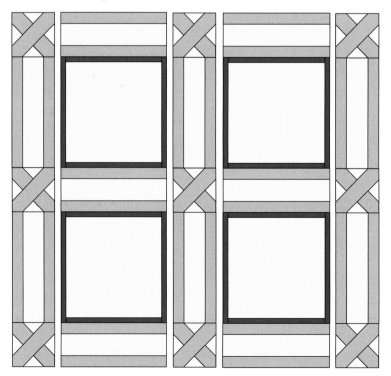

Border

1. Sew one 1" wide purple border strip to each of the four sides of the center assembly. Trim.

2. Sew one 2" x 37" plaid strip on each of two opposite outer edges of the purple border strips. Trim.

3. Sew one 2" x 40½" plaid strip on each of the two remaining sides of the center assembly.

4. Place the right sides together of one side of the center assembly and one 4½" x 40½" vine-print outer border strip. Sew.

5. Repeat Step 4 for the opposite side of the center assembly.

6. Place the right sides of an open side of the center assembly and one of the 4½" x 48" vine-print strips together. Sew, then press.

Quilt

1. Layer the muslin backing fabric, batting and pieced top.

2. Quilt by stitching in the ditch.

3. Quilt the fruit print areas by stitching outlines.

Bind

1. Join the six 2" wide purple strips end to end.

2. Bind the quilt. See Chapter 1 for instructions.

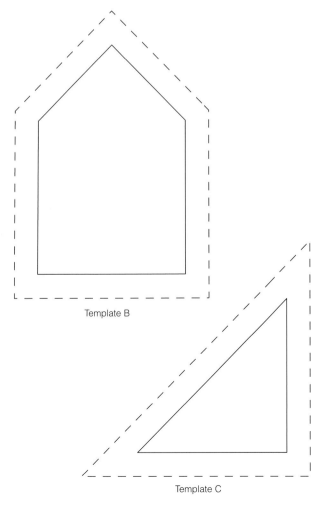

Template B

Template C

Fruit Table Runner.
Size: 16½" x 45".
Designed by Cheryl Adam.

Fruit Table Runner

This clever runner can double as an accent for your buffet serving area.

Materials

- 1½ yd. plain muslin
- ⅓ yd. beige solid
- ⅓ yd. purple solid
- ¼ yd. leafy print
- ¼ yd. fruit print
- 20" x 49" batting
- Thread

From	Cut
Fruit print	4 squares, 6¼" x 6¼"

Beige solid	2 squares, 10¾" x 10¾", cut twice diagonally to yield:
	    • 8 triangles
	2 squares, 5⅝" x 5⅝", cut twice diagonally to yield:
	    • 8 triangles

Purple solid	3 selvage-to-selvage strips, 2" wide
	4 selvage-to-selvage strips, 1" wide, cut to yield:
	    • 8 strips, 6¼" long
	    • 4 strips, 8¼" long
	    • 2 strips, 1" x 38"
	    • 2 strips, 1" x 10¾"

Leafy print	2 rectangles, 3¼" x 38½" 2 strips, 3¼" x 16½" strips
Plain muslin	1 rectangle, 20" x 49"

Assemble

Center blocks

1. Sew one 1" x 6¼" purple strip to each of two opposite sides of a 6¼" fruit print center square.

2. Sew one 1" x 8¼" purple strip to each of the remaining opposite sides of the fruit panel square.

3. Repeat Steps 1 and 2 for the remaining three fruit print center squares.

4. Arrange the beige side and corner triangles as shown in the diagram.

5. Sew the triangles to the squares.

Inner Border

1. Sew one 1" x 38" purple strip to each of the long sides of the center assembly.

2. Sew one 1" x 10¾" strip to each of the remaining short ends of the center assembly.

Outer Border

1. With the right side matched to the purple border, sew one 3¼" x 38½" leafy print outer border strip to each of the long sides of the center assembly.

2. Sew one 3¼" x 16½" strip to each of the short sides of the center assembly. Press.

Quilt

1. Layer the backing, batting and pieced top.

2. Quilt by stitching in the ditch.

3. Quilt the fruit print areas by stitching outlines.

Bind

1. Join three 2" purple strips.

2. Bind the table runner. See Chapter 1 for details on binding.

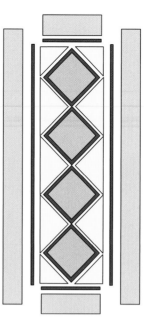

Table runner assembly diagram.

Kitchen Accessories

Toaster Cover

Keep your toaster looking tidy with this 6" x 7" x 11" cover.

Materials
- ⅛ yd. fruit print
- ¼ yd. heat-reflective fabric
- Thread

From	Cut
Fruit print	2 rectangles, 6½" x 25" 4 rectangles, 7½" x 11½"
Heat-reflective fabric	1 rectangle, 6" x 24" 2 rectangles, 7½" x 11½"

Assemble
1. With the fruit fabric right side out, place the 6" x 24" heat-reflective fabric rectangle between the two 6½" x 25" fruit print rectangles.
2. Quilt the layers together.
3. Repeat Steps 1 and 2 for the 7½" x 11½" side pieces.
4. With the right sides together, match the edges of one side piece to the long side of the large rectangle. Pin.
5. Sew with a ½" seam allowance.
6. Repeat Steps 4 and 5 for the opposite side piece.
7. Turn the finished piece right side out.

Potholders

Complete your kitchen decor with these 8" potholders.

Materials

- ¼ yd. fruit fabric
- ¼ yd. heat-resistant fabric
- 1 yd. double-fold bias tape, 1" wide
- Thread
- Water glass

From	Cut
Fruit fabric	2 squares, 8" x 8"
Heat-resistant fabric	1 square, 8" x 8"

Assemble

1. With right sides of the two fruit fabric squares facing out, insert one square of heat-resistant fabric between the squares.

2. Quilt the layers together.

3. Place a round object, such as a plastic water glass, at one corner of the quilted piece. Mark a half-circle at the outermost edge. This will be your cutting guide to round the corners.

4. Repeat Step 3 for the remaining corners.

5. Trim the corners along the line.

6. Wrap wide bias tape over the raw edges, extending the bias tape 2" at the beginning and at the end.

7. Topstitch through all layers along the inner fold of the bias tape, including the 2" extensions.

8. Create a loop by overlapping the bias tape extensions. Stitch through the layers to secure the loop.

Oven Mitt

Protect your hand with this 6" x 10" mitt.

Materials

- ¼ yd. fruit print
- ¼ yd. heat-reflective fabric
- 1 yd. cream double-fold bias tape, ½" wide
- Thread

From	Cut
Fruit print fabric	4 mitts (use the template)
Heat-reflective fabric	2 mitts (use the template)

Assemble

1. With the right sides out, match two fruit print mitts.

2. Place a heat-reflective fabric mitt piece between the two fruit print pieces.

3. Quilt the layers together.

4. Repeat Steps 1 through 3 for the other set of mitt pieces.

5. Sew wide bias tape along the lower edges of the mitt pieces.

6. With right sides out, match the two quilted mitt pieces. Pin.

7. Sew the mitt pieces together, using a ½" seam allowance along the side seams.

8. Wrap the bias tape along the unfinished edges. Extend one end of the tape to create a loop.

9. Sew through all layers and onto the extended bias tape.

10. Form a loop with the extra bias tape. Sew it in place.

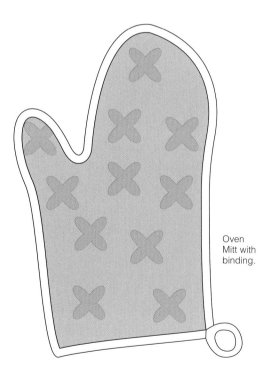

Oven Mitt with binding.

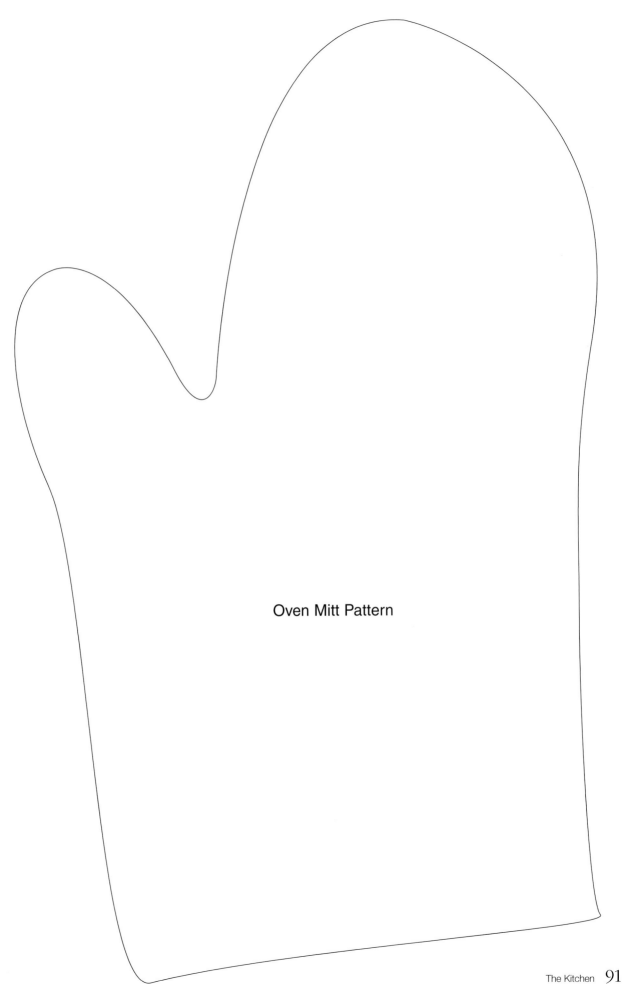

Oven Mitt Pattern

Bread/Casserole Warmer.
Size: 9" x 13".

Bread/Casserole Warmer

Keep bread and casseroles toasty with this easy-to-sew piece.

Materials

- ½ yd. fruit fabric
- ½ yd. heat-reflective fabric
- 2¼ yd. cream double-fold bias tape, ½" wide
- Thread

Variation

The directions yield a 9" x 13" pan warmer. Adjust the pattern to create a custom-size piece.

From	Cut
Fruit Fabric	2 rectangles, 14" x 18"
Heat-reflective fabric	1 rectangle, 14" x 18"

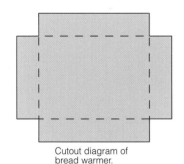

Cutout diagram of bread warmer.

Bias tape application.

Assemble

1. With the right sides facing out, match the fruit fabric rectangles together.

2. Insert the rectangle of heat-reflective fabric between the fruit fabric rectangles.

3. Quilt the layers together.

4. Cut away a 2½" square from all four corners.

5. At the inside corners, wrap double-fold bias tape over the raw edges, easing through the corner. Pin.

6. Topstitch through all of the layers along the inner fold of the bias tape.

7. Repeat Step 6 for the remaining corners.

8. Wrap double-fold bias tape over the long raw edge of the rectangle. Encase the ends of the bias tape applied in Step 5. Leave 3" extra at each corner.

9. Topstitch through the bias tape and all of the quilted piece's layers. Finish at the end of the overhanging bias tape.

10. Repeat Steps 8 and 9 for the remaining sides.

11. Tie the bias-tape ends together to form the warmer,

Place Mats

Complete your table with place mats.

Materials (for two place mats)
- ¾ yd. gold solid
- ⅝ yd. fusible fleece
- 3⅓ yd. gold double-fold bias tape, ½" wide
- Thread
- Water glass
- Fabric marker

From	Cut
Gold solid	4 rectangles, 12" x 18"
Fusible fleece	2 rectangles, 12" x 18"

Assemble

1. With the fruit fabric right side out, insert one fleece rectangle between two fruit fabric rectangles.
2. Quilt the layers together.
3. Place a round object, such a water glass, at one corner. Trace a half-circle around the glass at the outside edge of the fabric. Repeat for the remaining corners.
4. Trim the corners along the line.
5. Wrap the bias tape over the raw edges, overlapping at the beginning and end.
6. Topstitch through all layers along the inner fold.
7. Repeat Steps 1 through 6 for the other place mat.

Napkins

Fabric napkins add easy elegance.

Materials (for four napkins)
- 1 yd. fruit fabric
- 1 yd. vine print fabric
- Thread

From	Cut
Fruit fabric	4 squares, 15¼" x 15¼"
Vine print fabric	4 squares, 15¼" x 15¼"

Assemble

1. With right sides out, match one fruit square to one vine print square.
2. Use a serger or rolled hem foot to make a ¼" hem along the four sides of the fabric.
3. Repeat Steps 1 and 2 for the remaining napkins.

Donna's Favorite Family Recipes

Here's a taste of home from my table to yours. Enjoy these time-tested favorites with your friends and family.

Dewberry Pasta Salad

- 16-ounce box of bow tie or twisted pasta
- 2 cans, 10 ounces each, of white, boneless chicken or one medium-size whole chicken, freshly cooked and shredded
- 1 cup of mayonnaise
- 16-ounce jar of chunky-style salsa
- Everglades Seasoning
- Salt
- Pepper

Cook pasta until tender; follow the directions on the package. Drain pasta. Drain the shredded chicken, and add it to the pasta. Stir in the mayonnaise and salsa. Season to taste with Everglades Seasoning, salt and pepper. Serve hot or cold.

Donna's Potato Salad

- 10 pounds of potatoes
- 12 eggs
- 1 cup of celery, finely chopped
- 2 medium-size sweet onions, chopped
- 1 quart of mayonnaise
- 2 to 3 tablespoons of pickle relish
- 1 tablespoon of mustard
- 1 tablespoon of Everglades Seasoning
- Salt, to taste
- Pepper, to taste
- Paprika, to taste

Boil eggs. Peel and cut potatoes into bite-sized pieces; boil potatoes until tender in a pot of salted water. Drain the potato pieces, and transfer them to a bowl. Chop celery and onions; add them to the potatoes. Peel and slice the boiled eggs. Set aside a few slices to use as a garnish, and add the remainder to the potato pieces. Blend mayonnaise, mustard, relish, Everglades Seasoning, salt and pepper. Gently blend the mixture and potato pieces until well mixed, taking care to avoid breaking egg slices and potato pieces. Garnish the finished salad with reserved egg slices and paprika.

Tip: For a smaller family or gathering, reduce the recipe by half.

Seven-Layer Salad

- 1 head of iceberg lettuce, cut into thin strips
- ½ cup of bacon bits, or six slices of fresh-cooked bacon
- 1 cup chopped celery
- 2 cups mayonnaise
- 8-ounce can of sliced water chestnuts
- 1 teaspoon of sugar or Splenda sugar substitute
- 1 cup of diced tomatoes
- 1 cup of frozen peas, defrosted
- 4 ounces of grated sharp Cheddar cheese
- 1 onion, sliced
- 2 teaspoons of Everglades Seasoning, or to taste

Layer lettuce, celery, water chestnuts, peas, tomatoes, onions and bacon in a trifle bowl. Blend together mayonnaise, sugar and Everglades Seasoning. Spread mayonnaise, sugar and seasoning mixture over the top of layered salad. Garnish salad with cheese. Cover and chill for about 6 hours.

Chicken Crescents

- 2 packages, 16 ounces each, of refrigerated crescent rolls
- 1 stick of butter
- 2 cans, 10 ounces each, boneless white chicken
- 1 teaspoon of Everglades Seasoning
- 16 ounces of cream cheese
- 1 cup chopped celery
- 1 cup chopped onion
- ½ teaspoon garlic salt
- Dash of Pepper
- 1 can, 10 to 12 ounces, of cream of chicken soup

Using a skillet, sauté the celery and onions in butter. Add the chicken and the cream cheese; stir until well blended. Add Everglades Seasoning, garlic salt and pepper to taste. Unroll and separate the crescent roll triangles. Pull the dough away from the center to enlarge triangles. Spoon the chicken mixture into center of each crescent roll triangle. Fold each triangle's corners toward the center to cover the chicken mixture. Bake in 350-degree oven about 10 minutes, or until golden brown. Heat the soup without any added milk or water; use it as a gravy over the crescent rolls.

Fruit Dip

- 14 ounces of marshmallow cream
- 16 ounces of cream cheese, softened

Mix the marshmallow cream and cream cheese using a hand mixer. Serve with sliced fruit, such as strawberries, bananas, apples, cantaloupe and grapes.

- **Tip:** To keep fruits like apples and bananas from turning brown, dip pieces in pineapple or lemon juice, or clear citrus soda.

Variation

Add ½ cup of cranberries to the dip mix.

Black and White Cake

Crust:
- 1 cup all-purpose flour
- ½ cup butter, softened
- 1 cup chopped walnuts

Filling:
- 8-ounce package of cream cheese
- 1 cup of granulated sugar
- 6 ounces of whipped topping
- 3-ounce package of instant chocolate pudding
- 3-ounce package of instant vanilla pudding
- 3 cups cold milk

Topping:
- 6 ounces of whipped topping
- Grated chocolate

Mix the crust ingredients; spread mixture in the bottom of a 9" x 13" pan. Bake crust in 350-degree oven for 15 to 20 minutes. Allow crust to cool completely before adding filling.

Prepare the first layer of filling by blending cream cheese, sugar and whipped topping. Spread filling over the baked, cooled crust. In medium bowl, blend chocolate pudding mix with 1½ cups of milk until smooth. Set aside. In another medium bowl, blend vanilla pudding mix and 1½ cups of milk until smooth. Set aside. Spread all of the chocolate pudding on top of the cream cheese layer, then follow with all of the vanilla pudding on top of the chocolate pudding layer. Keep the layers separated so layering effect occurs. Top the vanilla pudding layer with remaining 6 ounces of whipped topping. Garnish with grated chocolate.

Banana Split Dessert
- 14-ounce box of graham crackers
- 2 cans, 20 ounces each, crushed pineapple
- 3 sticks of butter
- 4 to 5 bananas
- 2 teaspoons of granulated sugar
- 1 16-ounce jar of maraschino cherries
- 2 pounds of confectioners' sugar
- 16-ounce container of whipped topping
- 1 teaspoon of vanilla extract
- 2 teaspoons of milk
- Pecans (optional)

Crust: Crush graham crackers into crumbs. Blend graham cracker crumbs, granulated sugar and one stick of melted butter. Press mixture into a baking dish. If desired, bake crust for 10 minutes in a 350-degree oven, but allow crust to cool before adding filling.

Filling: Blend two sticks of softened butter with confectioners' sugar; beat until smooth. Add vanilla and milk, and mix well. Pour filling over graham cracker crust. Peel and slice bananas in half lengthwise, and place them over the mixture in the baking dish. Drain the crushed pineapple and spread over the bananas.

Top with a thick layer of whipped topping. Decorate finished dessert with cherries and pecans.

Chapter

Child's Room

Dancing Daisies and Butterflies Quilt.
Size: 63" x 84"; fits a standard twin bed.
Designer: Marsha Evans Moore.

Dancing Daisies and Butterflies Quilt

Create a sweet child's bed with accent shams and pillows. This sampler quilt is reminiscent of traditional style, but fresh fabrics give it a contemporary feel.

Materials

- 5 yd. coordinating fabric for backing
- 4½ yd. Flower Party Decorator Double border
- 2 yd. Flower Party Quilt Panels
- 2 yd. Small Tossed Flowers print
- 1¼ yd. Flower Patch print
- ½ yd. pink gingham
- ½ yd. cream solid
- ¼ yd. yellow solid
- ⅛ yd. green gingham
- ⅛ yd. green solid
- Twin-size batting, 72" x 90"
- Thread
- 10" dinner plate

From	Cut
Cream solid	2 squares, 10½" x 10½" 4 rectangles, 6¼" x 12"
Green gingham	16 blades (use Dresden Plate Blade template; add ¼" seam allowance)

Pink gingham	16 blades (use Dresden Plate Blade template; add ¼" seam allowance)
	5 selvage-to-selvage strips, 1½" wide, cut to yield:
	    • 4 strips, 10½" long
	    • 4 strips, 12½" long
	    • 4 strips, 14½" long
	2 bias-cut strips, 1" x 17"

Quilt Panels	1 center panel motif, 15" x 25" (fussy cut)
	Remaining center panel and border pieces (fussy cut) to yield:
	    • 2 flower pairs
	    • 2 single flowers
	    • 1 green gingham butterfly square, 7¾" x 7¾"
	    • 1 green gingham double flower face square, 7¾" x 7¾"
	    • 2 green gingham flower outline squares, 5¼" x 5¼"
	    • 4 plain green gingham rectangles, 3" x 4½"
	    • 2 pink gingham small butterfly rectangles, 4½" x 5¼"
	    • 3 pink gingham flower squares, 4½" x 4½"
	    • 3 pink gingham butterfly squares, 4½" x 4½"
	    • 1 pink gingham flower face square, 8½" x 8½"
	    • 1 pink gingham butterfly square, 8½" x 8½"

From	Cut

Yellow solid	2 rectangles, 2½" x 7¾"
	2 rectangles, 3¼" x 9"
	3 squares, 4½" x 4½", cut in half diagonally twice to yield:
	    • 12 triangles
	11 squares, 2½" x 2½", cut in half diagonally to yield:
	    • 22 triangles

Green solid	3 squares, 4½" x 4½", cut in half diagonally twice to yield:
	    • 12 triangles
	11 squares, 2½" x 2½", cut in half diagonally to yield:
	    • 22 triangles

Flower Patch print	6 squares, 4½" x 4½" (2 patches wide by 2 patches tall)
	2 strips, 2¼" x 16½" (8 patches wide by 1 patch tall)
	2 strips, 2¼" x 10" (6 patches wide by 1 patch tall)
	18 squares, 2½" x 2½" (each square is one patch)
	1 square, 8½" x 8½" (4 patches wide by 4 patches tall), cut in half diagonally to yield:
	    • 2 triangles (basket base)
	2 squares, 2½" x 2½", cut in half diagonally to yield:
	    • 4 triangles (basket base)

Small Tossed Flowers print	2 strips, 3" x 64" (cut lengthwise)
	2 strips, 3" x 34¾" (cut lengthwise)
	1 selvage-to-selvage strip, 1½" wide, cut to yield:
	    • 2 strips, 17½" long
	    • 2 strips, 27½" long
	2 selvage-to-selvage strips, 2" wide

Decorator Double Border	2 strips, 12¼" x 86" (with one edge at the green check) 2 strips, 12¼" x 65" strips (with one edge at the green check)
Backing fabric	2 rectangles, 14" x 88" (side panels) 1 rectangle, 41" x 88" (center panel)

Assemble

Center Panel Section A

1. Sew one 1½" x 27½" Tossed Flowers print strip to each of the long sides of the center panel.

2. Sew one 1½" x 17½" Tossed Flowers print strip to each of the short sides of the center panel.

Dresden Plate Blocks

1. Sew eight blades together, alternating colors, to form a plate.

2. Repeat Step 1 until all of the blades are sewn into plates.

3. Center a completed plate on a 10½" cream square. Pin.

4. Turn the curved outer edges under. Use satin stitching to appliqué the Dresden Plate to one cream square.

5. Apply fusible web to the wrong side of one single flower motif.

6. Remove the backing, and position the single flower piece over the center of the plate. Fuse the flower to the block.

7. Use a hem stitch or blanket stitch to topstitch along the edge of the flower.

8. Repeat Steps 2 through 7 for the remaining plates.

9. Sew one 1½" x 10½" pink gingham sashing strip to each of two opposite sides of the plate section.

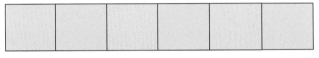

10. Sew one 1½" x 12½" pink gingham sashing strip to each of the remaining two sides. Press.

11. Sew one 2¼" x 12½" strip of the flower-motif gingham squares to the top edge of the plate section.

12. Arrange four 2½" squares on point with eight 2½" green triangles. Use squares cut in half diagonally to form triangles for the outer corners.

13. Sew the squares and triangles as shown.

14. Trim the finished piece to measure 3" x 12½".

15. Sew the bottom on-point squares section to the bottom of the plate section.

16. Repeat Steps 3 through 15 for the second Dresden Plate block.

Basket Block Handles

1. Mark a half-circle guideline for the handle on each of two 6¼" x 12" cream rectangles. Use a 10" dinner plate as a template.

2. Place the 1" x 17" pink gingham bias strip on the line. Trim to fit.

3. Pin in place.

4. Topstitch along both edges.

Basket Block Flowers

1. Apply fusible web to the wrong side of a flower and leaves motif.

2. Peel the paper. Position the piece under the center of the handle. Fuse it to the block.

3. Topstitch along the edge of the flower; using a hem stitch or blanket stitch.

4. Repeat Steps 1 through 3 for the remaining basket block.

Basket

1. Diagonally center one of the Flower Patch print basket base triangles on a 6½" x 12" cream rectangle.

2. Place two gingham triangles (with flower motif squares cut in half diagonally) on the base area of the basket.

3. Topstitch the triangle from Step 1 and the two triangles from Step 2 to the base area of the basket.

4. Sew the handle and basket sections along the centerline. Press.

5. Sew one pink gingham 1½" x 12½" strip to each of two opposite sides of the basket section.

6. Sew one pink gingham 1½" x 14½" strip to each of the remaining two sides of the basket section.

7. Repeat Steps 1 through 6 for the remaining basket section.

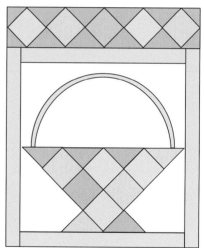

Basket block diagram.

Top Section of the Basket Blocks

1. Arrange the five 2½" Flower Patch print squares on point with the green background triangles.

2. Sew the squares and the triangles together.

3. Trim the block to 3¼" x 14". Use large triangles for the ends to fill out the space. Trim the excess.

4. Sew this five on-point square assembly to the top edge of the basket block.

5. Repeat Steps 1 through 4 for the second on-point square section.

Side Block B

Three On-Point Square Sections

1. Sew one quarter-square green triangle to each corner of one 4½" (four-square) block.

2. Sew one quarter-square yellow triangle to each corner of one 4½" (four-square) block.

3. Repeat Step 2.

4. Arrange the three assembled blocks from Steps 1 through 3 in a row, with the green triangle-accented square in the middle.

5. Sew the three squares together to form the on-point square unit.

6. Alternate three of the 4½" pink squares with two of the 2⅜" x 4½" green rectangles. Sew.

7. Sew the on-point square unit to the left side of the pink square and green rectangle section created in Step 4.

8. Sew one 2" x 7¼" yellow rectangle to one 8½" green square.

9. Sew one 2⅛" x 9½" Flower Patch print rectangle to the top of this section. The top of the section should have the yellow rectangle on the left.

10. Sew the top edge of the section created in Step 7 (top) to the bottom of the section created in Step 5.

11. Repeat Steps 1 through 10, but arrange the pieces so they form a mirror-image version of the first Section B block.

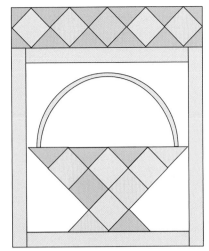

Basket block diagram.

On-point squares.

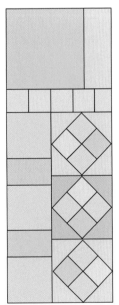
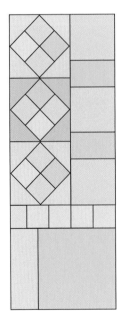

Section B.   Mirror Section B.

Join

Sections A and B

1. Arrange the Center Panel A between the Section B blocks.

2. Sew along the long seams.

3. Set aside.

Section C

1. Sew one 4½" x 5¼" Butterfly rectangle to one 5¼" green gingham-with-flower-outline square.

2. Sew one 3¼" x 9" plain yellow rectangle to the long side of the piece created in Step 1.

3. Sew one 7¾" green butterfly/double flower face square to the bottom of the section created in Step 2.

4. Sew one 1⅞" x 16½" Flower Patch print rectangle to the left side of the section created in Step 3.

5. Repeat Steps 1 through 4 for the second Section C. Use the remaining motif pieces.

End

1. Arrange one Section C with one Dresden Plate and one Basket block, as shown in the diagram

2. Sew the sections together.

3. Repeat Steps 1 and 2 with the remaining Section C, Dresden Plate and Basket blocks.

4. Arrange the center and lower sections as shown.

5. Sew the sections together.

6. Sew the remaining end section to the joined middle and end sections.

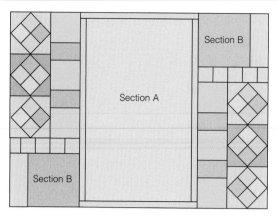

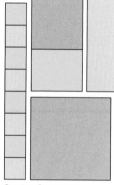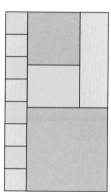

Section C assembly.

Completed Section C.

End section assembly.

Middle and End Section assembly.

Inner Border

1. Sew the two 3" x 34¾" Tossed Flowers border strips to the opposite short sides of the completed center sections.

2. Sew the two 3" x 64" Tossed Flowers border strips to the two long sides of the center assembly.

Outer Border

1. With right sides together, center one 12¼" x 86" outer border strip along one long side of the pieced top. Pin. The border will extend evenly beyond both ends of the top for the mitered corner.

2. Sew to the side, beginning and ending ¼" from the corners.

3. Repeat Steps 1 and 2 for the remaining long side.

4. Center a 12¼" x 65" border fabric strip along one of the short sides of the pieced top. Pin.

5. Sew to the side, beginning and ending ¼" from the corners.

6. Repeat Steps 4 and 5 for the second side.

7. Miter the corners by folding the border fabric at a 45-degree angle at the corners. Finger press.

8. Match the finger-pressed diagonal folds. Pin.

9. Sew along the 45-degree fold.

10. Trim the extra fabric, ¼" from the stitching.

11. Repeat Steps 7 through 10 for the remaining three corners.

Quilt

1. Place the batting between the assembled top and the back.

2. Lightly quilt through all the layers in the ditch along the seam lines.

3. Outline quilt around the flower and leaf motifs.

Bind

1. Join the 2" wide Tossed Flower strips end to end.

2. Bind the quilt. See Chapter 1 for instructions.

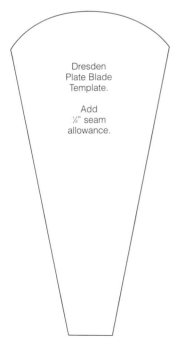

Dresden
Plate Blade
Template.

Add
¼" seam
allowance.

Keepsake Box.
Size: 10" x 12".

Keepsake Box

Hide your treasures in this easy-to-make chest.

Materials

- ½ yd. Flower Patch print
- 8½" x 10" piece of polyester quilt batting
- 2 yd. of ¼" wide double-stick fusible web
- 9½" x 11" piece of cardboard
- 10" x 12" x 4" hinged lid box with an 8½" x 10" opening
- Folk Art® Acrylic Colors paints in Sunflower 432, Thicket 924, Violet Pansy 514, Wicker White 901
- Folk Art® One Stroke™ Brushes No. 16 Flat, No. 12 Flat and No. 2 Script Liner
- Paint palette
- Fine-grit sandpaper
- Shipping tape, 2" wide
- 4 matching decorative drawer pulls, 1" diameter
- Spray lacquer
- Clear construction adhesive
- Pencil (optional)
- Fabric glue (optional)
- Embroidery ribbon (optional)
- Embroidery needle (optional)
- Tack cloth

From	Cut
Flower Patch print	1 rectangle, 9½" x 11"* *If the back side of the cardboard will be exposed with the box you are using, cut a second rectangle of fabric that is 2" larger.
Cardboard	Rectangle to fit in the frame
Batting	Rectangle to fit in the frame

Paint

Base Color

1. Sand the box to remove rough spots.

2. Clean the sanded box with a tack cloth.

3. Paint the box with two coats of Wicker White.

Vine and Leaves

1. Double load the No.16 Flat brush with Thicket and Sunflower paints. Add a touch of Wicker White to the Sunflower side. Blend well to soften.

2. With chisel edge of the brush, lead with the Sunflower/Wicker White side and pull a main vine around the sides. Add tendrils off of the main vine.

3. Use the flat side of the same brush and colors used in Step 2 to paint some One-Stroke leaves. Then use the chisel edge of the brush to pull a stem from the vine into the leaves.

Butterflies

1. Double load the No. 12 Flat brush with Violet Pansy and Wicker White.

2. Use the flat side of the brush, with the Violet Pansy to the outer edge, to paint butterfly wings.

3. Flip the brush so the Wicker White is on the outer edge. Paint a second wing for some butterflies.

4. Load the No. 2 Script Liner with inky-consistency Thicket. Touch the tip of the liner to the area of the head, apply slight pressure, and then slide the brush as you lift back to the tip to make the tail. Add the antennae and a few curlicues throughout the design to mimic new vine growth.

Seal

1. Allow the paint to dry completely.

2. Spray the box with one light coat of lacquer.

3. Allow the lacquer to dry completely.

4. Repeat Steps 2 and 3 to add two to three coats of lacquer.

Assemble

Padded Box Top

1. If desired, embellish the fabric that will cover the padded box top with ribbon embroidery.

2. Layer the batting on top of the cardboard and wrap the smaller fabric rectangle over the batting and cardboard. Pull the fabric around to the backside of the cardboard and use shipping tape to secure the raw fabric edges to the cardboard.

Interior Box Top Cover (optional)

1. Hem the second fabric rectangle to give a finished fabric look to the inside of the lid. Fold each edge over by ½". Press. Fold each edge over by ½" a second time. Press.

2. Use double-stick fusible web to secure the hem.

Finish

1. Secure the fabric-covered padded box top in the frame.

2. If desired, use fabric glue to attach the hemmed fabric rectangle so it covers the exposed cardboard or the inside of the box top.

3. Flip the box upside down. Use clear construction adhesive to secure the decorative drawer pulls on each corner of the bottom of the box.

Variations

• For a faster-to-finish project, simplify the decorative painting motif or paint the box a solid color that complements the fabric.

• Decoupage can add a custom decorative touch to the box.

Pillowcase

Fabric Requirements

- ¾ yd. Flower Patch print
- ¼ yd. accent fabric
- 1½ yd. rickrack in coordinating color
- Thread

See Chapter 10 for instructions.

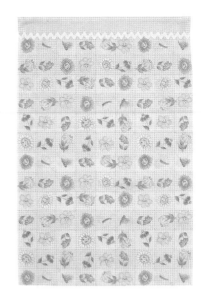

Pillow Sham

Fabric Requirements

- ¾ yard Small Tossed Flowers print
- Thread

See Chapter 10 for instructions.

Button Pillow

Fabric Requirements

- ½ yd. solid
- 1 Flower Party Quilt panel border square
- Thread
- Fusible fleece
- Button
- Pillow form

See Chapter 10 for instructions.

Decorator Table Covers

Fabric Requirements

- 2 yd. Small Packed Hydrangeas print
- 1 yd. Flower Party print
- Thread

See Chapter 10 for instructions.

The Guest Room

Bed of Roses Quilt.
Size: 54" x 75"; fits a full bed with a 15" drop.

Bed of Roses Quilt

Create a luxurious bed with accent shams and pillows. This dramatic quilt will lend elegance to your room. It has a center area lush with roses, a pieced border and a formal box-pleated skirt. The center panel/pieced top is quilted, while the skirt is left unlined.

Materials

- 4¼ yd. Donna's Roses Large Double Border print
- 2¼ yd. muslin, 60" wide
- 3 yd. pink small floral print
- 1⅜ yd. Large Packed Roses print
- 1¼ yd. white floral
- 1 yd. blue plaid
- 60" x 80" piece of thin polyester batting
- Thread

From	Cut
Packed Roses print	1 rectangle, 24½" x 48½"
Blue plaid	8 strips, 4½" x 40"
White floral	8 strips, 4½" x 40" 3 strips, 2" x 40"
Pink small floral print	1 lengthwise strip, 4½" x 108," cut to yield: • 16 squares, 4½" x 4½" 6 lengthwise strips, 1½" x 108," cut to yield: • 4 lengths, 12½" • 2 lengths, 24½" 4 lengthwise strips, 2" x 108," cut to yield: • 2 lengths, 50½"
Large Double Border print	Full yardage in half lengthwise along the fold. Cut each half to yield: • 1 strip, 15" x 64" • 2 strips, 15" x 84"
Muslin	1 rectangle, 60" x 80"

Assemble

Nine-Patch Blocks

1. Arrange the blue plaid, white floral and pink floral 4½" strips into sets as follows:

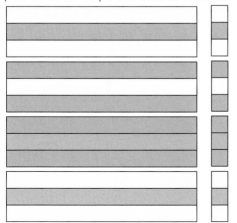

Assemble strip sets, then cut 4½" lengths.

2. With a ¼" seam allowance, sew the strip sets together lengthwise.

3. Press the seams to one side.

4. Cross cut the strips into 4½" lengths.

5. Repeat for the remaining strip sets.

6. With a pink square in the middle, arrange the three-block sets into nine-patches as illustrated.

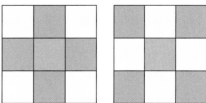

Assemble the nine-patch blocks.

7. Stitch the nine-patch blocks with opposing seams. Press.

Center Panel

1. With right sides together, sew one 1½" x 24½" pink sashing strip to each of the two shorter sides of the center panel.

2. Fold the sashing open to the right side. Press.

3. Sew two sets of two nine-patch blocks into pairs.

4. Sew each completed pair of nine-patch blocks to a short side of the center panel.

Center panel with inner sashing.

5. Sew one 1½" x 74½" pink sashing strip to each of the long sides of the center panel.

6. Sew two sets of four nine-patch sections into a four-block strip.

7. Sew one 1½" x 12½" pink sashing strip to each end of each four-block strip.

8. Sew one nine-patch block to each pink sashing strip at both ends of the four patch strips.

9. Sew the units from Step 8 to the long sides of the center panel.

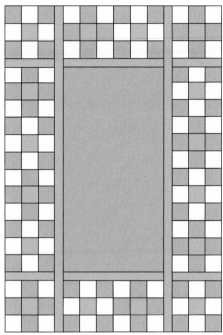

Completed center assembly.

Outline Border

1. Sew one 2" x 50½" pink sashing strip to each short side of the center assembly.

2. Sew one 2" x 50½" pink sashing strip to each long side of the center assembly.

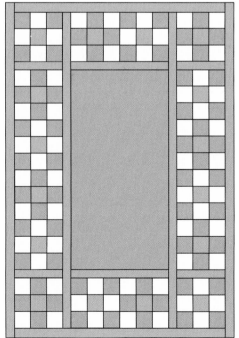

Outer sashing diagram.

Quilt

1. Layer the batting between the assembled top and the muslin.
2. Lightly quilt along the seam lines; quilt through all of the layers.
3. Trim the layers evenly. Zigzag stitch or serge along the outer raw edges.

Add Skirt

1. Sew the 64" center panel of the skirt between the two longer side panels.
2. With right sides together, match one end of the skirt with the assembled top.
3. Pin along the side to the corner of the top.
4. Fold the skirt fabric back onto itself.
5. Fold the fabric back again to the point where the seam meets the corner of the assembled top.
6. Pin the pleat to the corner.
7. Turn the corner. Pin the skirt fabric to the top for the same distance as in the first half of the pleat.
8. Fold the fabric back onto itself to the point where it meets the previous fold at the center of the pleat.
9. Fold the fabric back onto itself along the front of the skirt.
10. Pin the second half of the pleat.
11. With right sides together, continue matching the raw edge of the skirt to the assembled top along the front side.
12. Repeat Steps 4 through 11 to form a second pleat. Stop pinning at this point.
13. Stitch the first side of the skirt along the pinned side, stopping ¼" from the corner.
14. Backstitch at the end.
15. Resume stitching along the front side of the skirt, stopping ¼" from the corner.
16. Backstitch and cut the thread.
17. Resume pinning the right sides of the skirt and assembled top, forming the second half of the pleat.
18. Stitch the remaining side of the skirt to the assembled top.

Bind

1. Join the three 2" wide white floral strips end to end.
2. Bind only the top edge of the quilt. See Chapter 1 for instructions.

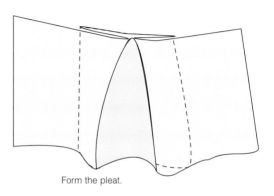

Form the pleat.

Album Cover

Dress up your favorite photographs with this project.

Materials

- ¼ yd. Large Packed Roses print
- ½ yd. Small Rosebuds print
- ⅛ yd. Small Packed Hydrangeas print
- 24" x 28" piece of batting
- Photo album, 9½" x 11"
- Spray adhesive
- Matching or neutral thread
- Embroidery needle (optional)
- 1 yd. pale shamrock silk ribbon (optional)
- 1 yd. bright yellow silk embroidery ribbon

Assemble

Front Panel

1. Stitch one 3½" pink corner square to each end of the two 11½" strips.

2. With right sides together, sew one 3" x 9" rosebud strip to each of the short sides of the center panel. Press the borders open.

3. With right sides together, sew one of the corner block strips to each of the long sides of the center panel.

4. If desired, embellish the center of the front panel with ribbon embroidery.

5. Place the piece of batting on the front of the album. Secure the batting with spray adhesive.

6. Center the front panel on the front of the album. Wrap the raw edges of the panel around the cover.

7. Fold the corners to form miters. Secure the corners with hot glue.

From	Cut
Packed Roses print	1 rectangle, 9" x 11½"
Small Rosebuds print	1 selvage-to-selvage strip, 3" wide 1 rectangle, 12" x 14" 2 rectangles, 9" x 12"
Packed Hydrangeas print	4 squares, 3½" x 3½"
Batting	2 rectangles, 12" x 14"

Back Cover

1. Complete the back cover, following Steps 6 through 8 from the Front Panel section. Use the 12" x 14" Donna's Roses rectangle.

Inside Covers

1. Fold the raw edges of a 9" x 12" rectangle so that the piece measures 8½" x 11" and has four finished edges. Press.

2. Center the panel on the inside front cover.

3. Secure the panel with hot glue.

4. Repeat Steps 1 through 3 for the inside back cover.

5. If desired, outline the center front panel with the silk ribbon, attaching it with hot glue.

Variation

Use fabrics to coordinate memory pages with the album cover.

Chapter

Accessories

Basic Pillow

Round out a room with this quick and easy pillow.

Materials (for a 14" square pillow)
- ½ yd. fabric
- Thread
- Pillow form

From
Fabric

Cut
1 square, 15" x 15"
2 rectangles, 10" x 15"

Pillow back pieces overlapped.

Stitching line.

Assemble
1. Fold ½" of fabric under on one long side of each rectangle. Topstitch.

2. With right sides together, layer the two 10" x 15" rectangles on the 15" x 15" square. Place the hems toward the center, overlapping as shown. Pin.

3. Stitch a ½" seam allowance around all four sides.

4. Press the seam allowances open.

5. Turn the piece right side out.

6. Topstitch ¼" from the outer edges to form a beaded edge.

7. Fit the finished pillow cover over the pillow form.

Variation
For a different look, use a printed panel for the front of the pillow. Follow the same directions for the Basic Pillow, except cut two back pieces that measure one half the width of the panel plus 5".

Button Pillow

Jazz up a basic pillow with this accent.

Materials

- Scrap of fleece
- 1 pink flower outline square from Flower Party Quilt Panel
- Scrap of fusible web
- Thread
- Completed Basic Pillow

Assemble

1. Complete a Basic Pillow.
2. Cut out the daisy shape from the Flower Party Quilt Panel.
3. Fuse the flower cutout to the fleece.
4. Sew a shank button through the center of the fused daisy and the Basic Pillow.

Flange Pillow

Flanges add a designer touch to this pillow.

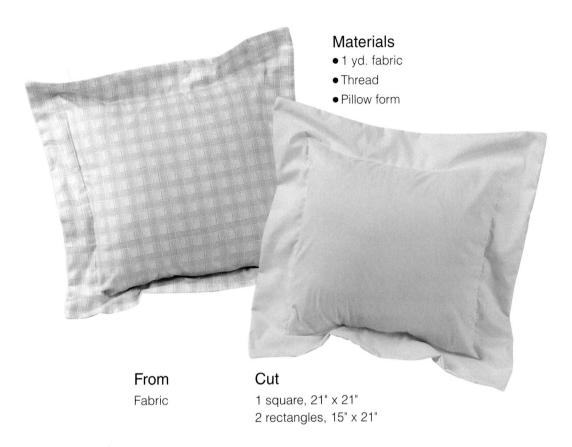

Materials
- 1 yd. fabric
- Thread
- Pillow form

From	Cut
Fabric	1 square, 21" x 21"
	2 rectangles, 15" x 21"

Assemble

1. Fold ½" of fabric under on one long side of each rectangle. Topstitch.

2. With right sides together, layer the two rectangles on the square piece. Place the hems toward the center. Pin.

3. Stitch a ½" seam allowance around all four sides.

4. Press the seam allowances flat.

5. Turn the piece right side out.

6. Topstitch 2½" from the outer edges to form a flange. Measure 2½" to the right of the sewing machine needle, and place a piece of tape as a guide.

7. Topstitch ¼" from the outer edges to form a beaded edge.

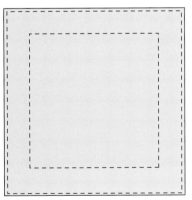

Plain flange pillow.

Chair Pillow

Fit for a princess, this cushion completes a charming setting.

Materials

- ¾ yd. fabric
- Package of fiberfill
- Long upholstery needle
- 2 shank buttons
- Pencil
- String
- Thread

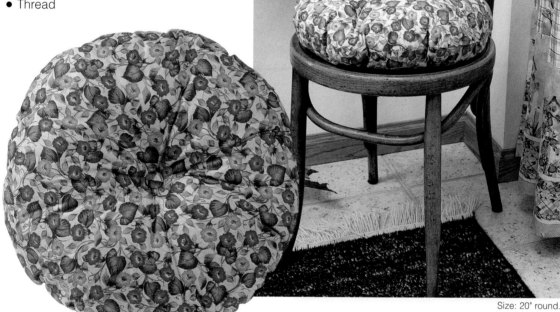

Size: 20" round.

From

Green floral

Cut

2 circles, 21" in diameter

Tip: To cut a circle, fold the piece of fabric in half, then in half again. Attach a 10½" length of string to a marking pencil. Pin the string to the corner at the folds. With the string taut, draw an arc on the fabric with the marking pencil. Cut through all layers on the arc line.

Assemble

1. With right sides together, match the two circles.
2. Sew with a ½" seam allowance, leaving a 5" opening.
3. Turn the piece right side out.
4. Stuff with fiberfill.
5. Sew the opening closed.

Tuft

1. Thread a long needle with doubled strong thread.
2. Sew one shank buttons to the center of each side of the pillow. Secure the thread with a hidden knot, then cut the thread.

Panel Pillow

Vary this pillow's look with flanges made from a contrasting fabric.

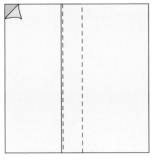

Materials

- 1 panel, 19½" square
- ⅔ yd. coordinating fabric
- ⅓ yd. accent fabric
- Thread
- Pillow form

From	Cut
Square panel	1 square, 19½" x 19½"
Floral or plaid	2 rectangles, 16" x 24"
Accent fabric	4 selvage-to-selvage strips, 2½" wide

Assemble

1. Sew one 2½" wide accent strip to each side of the front center panel.

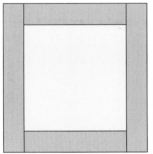

Sew the accent fabric to the center panel.

2. Fold under ½" of one long side of each 16" x 24" piece. Topstitch.

3. With right sides together, layer the two rectangles on the square. Place the hems toward the center. Overlap the pieces as shown. Pin.

Lay the two back pieces on the right side of the front.

Tip: To use panels of other sizes, cut two back pieces that each measure one half the width of the panel plus 5".

4. Use a ½" seam allowance, and stitch around all four sides.

5. Press the seam allowances flat. Turn the piece right side out.

6. Topstitch ¼" from the outer edge to finish the seam.

7. Topstitch 2½" from the outer edges to form a flange. Measure 2½" to the right of the sewing machine needle and place a piece of tape as a stitching guide.

8. Insert a pillow through the opening in the back.

Sew a ½" seam allowance.

Sew 2½" from the outer edge to form the flange.

Pillow Shams

Create a tailored look with these simple shams.

Materials
- 1½ yd. coordinating fabric
- Thread

From	Cut
Fabric	2 rectangles, 27" x 32"
	4 rectangles, 20" x 27"

Assemble

1. Fold under ½" of one long side of each 20" x 27" piece. Topstitch.

2. With right sides together, layer two 20" x 27" pieces on one 27" x 32" piece. Place the hems of the two pieces toward the center, and make sure they overlap. Pin.

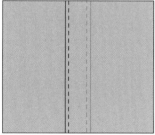

Layer the two back pieces on the right side of the front.

3. Using a ½" seam allowance, stitch around all four sides.

4. Press the seam allowances flat.

5. Turn the piece right side out.

Size: 26" x 31"

Finish

1. Topstitch 3" from the outer edges to form a flange. Measure 3" to the right of the sewing machine needle and place a piece of tape on the work surface to use as a guide.

2. Insert a pillow through the opening in the back.

3. Repeat the Assemble and Finish steps for a second sham.

topstitch 2½" from the outer edges

Accent Pillowcase

Complete a bed with a matching pillowcase.

Size: 20" x 30".

Materials (for one standard-size pillowcase)

- ¾ yd. print fabric
- ¼ yd. accent fabric
- 1⅛ yd. rickrack or lace (optional)
- Thread
- Serger (optional)

From	Cut
Print fabric	1 rectangle, 27" x 41"
Accent fabric	1 strip, 9" x 40"

Assemble

1. With right side out, fold the accent fabric rectangle in half lengthwise to form a cuff. Press.

2. With right sides together, match the folded cuff to the long side of the main section. Pin.

3. Using a ½" seam allowance, stitch the cuff in place.

4. Stitch over the raw edge with a serger or zigzag stitch.

5. Press the cuff open.

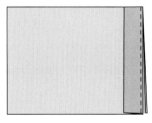

6. If desired, place the rickrack or lace over the seam. Topstitch in place.

7. With right sides together and matching the cuff seams, fold the assembled piece in half. Pin.

8. Using a ½" seam allowance, stitch the side and bottom seams.

9. Zigzag stitch the raw edge, or use a serger to sew over the raw edge.

10. Turn right side out. Press.

Valance

Round out a room with a coordinating valance.

Size: Finished length 12" to 18" x 72" (for a 36" wide window).

Materials

- 2 yd. border print
- Thread

From	Cut
Border print	1 strip, 16" x 72"

Tip: Make valances twice the inner width of the window to ensure adequate gathering.

Variation

Stitch an additional strip along the lower edge to make an additional border. You may want to insert a strip of coordinating solid fabric to create a striped effect.

Assemble

1. Stitch a ½" hem along the bottom and two sides of the border print strip.

2. At the top, fold 3" of fabric to the wrong side.

3. Turn ½" under at the raw edge and pin along the fold.

4. Topstitch along the fold. Press.

5. Place a line of stitching 1½" from the top fold.

6. To form the rod pocket, place a second line of stitching 3" from the top fold.

Decorator Table Covers

Add a chic touch to a side table.

Materials

- 4 yd. coordinating fabric
- 1 yd. contrasting fabric
- 1 yd. string
- Marking pencil
- Thread
- Serger (optional)

From	Cut
Coordinating fabric	2 halves, each 72" long
Contrasting fabric	1 square, 36" x 36"

Size: Base layer, 70" diameter;
Top layer, 36" square.

Assemble

Circular Cloth

1. Match the right sides of the two 72" lengths of coordinating fabric. Stitch a ½" seam along the selvages.
2. Open the seam. Press.
3. Fold the piece in half and in half again.
4. Attach a 36" length of string to a marking pencil.
5. Pin the string to the corner at the folds.
6. With the string taut, draw an arc on the fabric with the marking pencil.
7. Cut through all layers on the arc line.
8. Serge or hem the curved edge.

Square Top

1. Serge or hem the 36" square.

Contributors and Resources

Contributors

"Donna Dewberry's Complete Book of One-Stroke Painting," North Light Books, 1998.

Materials

Dewberry Designs Inc.
365 Citrus Tower Blvd., Suite 106
Clermont, FL 34711
(352) 394-7344
http://www.onestroke.com

Everglades Seasoning
Everglades Foods Inc.
P.O. Box 595
La Belle, FL 33975
(800) 689-2221

Prym-Dritz Corp.
Sewing, quilting and craft-related notions
P.O. Box 5028
Spartanburg, SC 29304
http://www.prymdritz.com

Springs Creative Products Group
P.O. Box 10232
Rock Hill, SC 29731
(800) 234-6688
http://www.springscreativeproductsgroup.com/

Project Designers

Cheryl Adam
e-mail: cheryl.adam@verizon.net

Cheryl Adam is a quilt designer, author and teacher. Her Dresden Plate Quilt is a traditional pattern made with a fresh block arrangement. Appliquéd flowers embellish her Purple Porch Throw.

Marsha Evans Moore
e-mail: memoore1043@aol.com

Marsha Evans Moore is a professional quilt designer whose special interests include antique and traditional quilt designs. A 19th century sampler inspired her for the Dancing Daisies and Butterflies Quilt design.

Julie A. Olson
e-mail: hugsandstitches@means.net

Julie Olson is a quilt pattern designer, teacher and lecturer. The fabrics inspired her to make a medallion quilt using the pillow panel for the center. The picket fence made a natural border.

Michele Crawford
Web site: http://www.flowerboxquilts.com

Michele Crawford is a published quilt designer, teacher and lecturer. The smiling daisies in the fabric inspired her Baby Quilt. The light, fresh colors evoke a look that's perfect for the nursery.

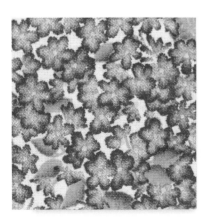